PUFFIN BOOKS

Editor: Kaye Webb

CW01667321

Nowhere to Stop

Christmastime, and nowhere to go, not for gypsies anyway. When there was no more fruit for them to pick or farm work to be done no one wanted Liberty Lovell and his family. Even if they only wanted to stop on a town dump for a few days, they encountered indignant householders and surly policemen.

At first Chris and his friends didn't want them either. The dump was *their* place. They'd made a hideout there. Chris even threw a stone through the window of the caravan when Liberty's mother screeched at his sister. Then there was a crash and the tinkle of glass and a long wail like the howl of a wolf . . .

'I shouldn't have chucked that stone,' muttered Chris.

'Going to have a baby, wasn't she?' said June, as if she knew all about it. 'Might be born at Christmas.' Chris stared at her and his face went white. A baby coming, frost everywhere, and snow due on the forecast.

After that he *wanted* the gypsies to stay, but it wasn't easy to arrange, especially with Tom's busybodying mother drumming up a petition to get them moved.

For readers of nine and over.

GERALDINE KAYE

Nowhere to stop

Illustrated by Gareth Floyd

Puffin Books

Puffin Books,
Penguin Books Ltd,
Harmondsworth, Middlesex, England
Penguin Books, 625 Madison Avenue,
New York, New York 10022, U.S.A.
Penguin Books Australia Ltd,
Ringwood, Victoria, Australia
Penguin Books Canada Ltd,
41 Steelcase Road West, Markham, Ontario, Canada
Penguin Books (N.Z.) Ltd,
182–190 Wairau Road, Auckland 10, New Zealand

First published by Brockhampton Press 1972
Published in Puffin Books 1974
Reprinted 1977

Made and printed in Great Britain by
Richard Clay (The Chaucer Press) Ltd, Bungay, Suffolk
Set in Linotype Pilgrim

Contents

I On the dump

'I bet today is the coldest day since the Thames froze and that's three hundred years,' Chris said, and Tom was inclined to agree.

'Bet it's colder at the North Pole,' said Dusty.

'You don't half look funny,' Tom said. Dusty's face was quite white and his round nose was like a blue marble.

'Funny yourself,' Dusty snapped. 'What's the point standing here like fish fingers? Let's go home.'

The three boys stood at the corner of the High Street with their coat collars turned up and their hands in their pockets. A bit of newspaper scraped along the gutter in the icy wind. It was Sunday afternoon and the High Street was deserted, but somewhere round behind the houses the Salvation Army was playing *Hark the Herald Angels Sing*.

'Let's go and find them?' said Tom.

'Let's go home,' said Dusty.

'Let's go round the dump,' said Chris. 'I've got an idea.' When Chris gets an idea his eyes go bright, brown, and shiny like new conkers.

There used to be a big house on the dump once. They pulled it down years ago but you can still find bits of brick in the grass and there's an old apple tree and a stone wall all round that was the garden wall. It's great in the summer, except that everybody throws things on the dump.

In the winter there's nothing much but old boxes and tins and mud.

'Round the dump? Don't call that an idea do you?' Dusty said, but already they were halfway down Kings' Street to the old boarded-up shops where you get on to the dump.

Chris's ideas are like that, only Dusty was thinking about buttered crumpets for tea and how his ears were nearly falling off. Tom was thinking of home too, about his mum who never let them have the telly on on a Sunday. 'Sunday is Sunday in this house,' she says. Besides that there was his sister Mary, practising gentle smiles in the mirror because she wanted to be Mary in the school play. So Tom wasn't particular about going home just yet.

The three boys went between the boarded-up shops on to the dump and stood looking at the old boxes and the mud and the grey backs of the houses and the big square block that was West Flats on the other side.

'It's blinkin' cold,' said Dusty, and his teeth chattered.

'What we want is a den,' said Chris with his eyes all bright. 'We could make a den against the wall and there'd still be wood left over for a lovely fire. I got some matches. Might roast potatoes even,' he added dreamily.

'Where we going to get potatoes?' said Tom, but already they were dragging boxes over to the wall.

'It's a place of our own, see?' said Chris, 'and nobody else is going to come unless we say.'

'How we going to stop them, electric fence?' said Dusty sarcastically.

'Be lovely summertime,' said Chris. 'We might even live here summertime. Sleep and eat and everything.'

'Just see my mum letting me, can't you?' said Tom.

It was freezing cold on the dump but the boys were so

busy dragging boxes and bits of corrugated iron from all over the place that they forgot the cold. Tom found some long sticks from his dad's runner-beans and they put them across from the wall to the old apple tree.

They put corrugated iron on top of the sticks and that was the roof. The stone wall was one wall of the den already, and they used the boxes for another wall, big ones at the bottom and small ones at the top. That was two walls; but then there were only two boxes left and they couldn't finish.

'What's the use of a den with only two walls?' Tom shouted angrily. 'We got to have four blinkin' walls and wood for a fire.'

'Plenty of wood down the old airfield, isn't there?' said Chris.

'What old airfield?' said Dusty.

'It's not far,' said Chris, and his eyes were all bright again. 'There's lots of old huts and wood lying everywhere. All you got to do is pick it up. Only we'll have to have the barrow.' He looked sideways at Dusty because the barrow belonged to Dusty's Auntie Flo who had a stall in the market. Dusty went to help her every Saturday.

Dusty flicked his spectacles up his nose. 'No harm in asking, I suppose,' he said doubtfully.

'Don't want to bother asking people, Sunday afternoon,' said Chris. 'Probably having a snooze and her false teeth out on the table. Not going to want it Sunday afternoon, is she?'

'Well . . .' said Dusty.

Five minutes later the boys trundled the barrow up the High Street. 'It's a good barrow, this is,' Dusty said, rather pink because it was uphill. 'Don't make barrows like this nowadays.'

'Which way?' said Tom.

'Straight down the High Street and turn left and then left again and then right,' Chris said. 'It's about two miles.'

'You said two miles, two miles ago,' said Tom, and Chris took the barrow and swung it round the first left turn.

'Let's go back,' said Dusty. 'It's going to snow.'

Half an hour later the grey High Street was far behind and the houses had bits of lawn in front. And then the houses were wide apart with gardens all round and the boys turned another corner and there were no houses at all, only a narrow lane with black twiggy hedges.

The barrow rumbled on and nobody spoke. Tom looked up and the sky was a sort of violet colour and there was a single star.

'Let's go back,' Tom said. 'My mum'll do me if I'm late for tea.'

'Here we are then,' said Chris, and he swung the barrow through a gap in the hedge.

It was the old airfield. There was a great open space with long grass and a concrete runway going across it like a broad white ribbon. Some battered wooden huts squatted by the hedge, the roof-felt flapped and heaved in the wind. At the first hut there was a veranda and a notice-board, on which bits of yellow paper fluttered like frantic moths. 'Let's go home,' Dusty whispered.

'Give us a hand then,' said Chris.

It didn't take long to get the wood piled up. The boys pushed the barrow back to the road. Some of the wood fell off but they didn't stop because there were lots of stars now and the sky was inky blue.

'You need two to push,' gasped Chris because the barrow was heavy and he and Tom took a handle each. Then an owl hooted and Dusty's heart jumped like a trapped mouse, and he dived between the others. 'You need three to push,' he said.

It was quite dark when they got back to the High Street. The street-lights stretched away like strings of crystal beads. There wasn't much traffic.

'Downhill now,' said Dusty, and the barrow began to run on its own. More bits of wood fell off but the barrow went faster and faster. The boys' feet flew over the ground. They rattled past the shops and The Bull, and reached the terrace where Chris and Tom both lived. They shot past Chris's house, number twenty-one, and Chris's sister, June, who was coming out with the old dog, Rags. June shouted something but the boys didn't hear and they couldn't stop. They shot past number twenty-five, Tom's house, with an anxious glance at the net curtains, and then they were past the terrace and the Co-op and June was running after them. The traffic light at the corner was red but they still couldn't stop.

'Pull on the left,' Chris yelled out and they all three flung themselves on to the left handle and the barrow lurched round the corner and ran on down Kings' Street.

'Find ourselves in court, going against the lights,' Tom shouted.

'How we going to get her on the dump?' yelled Dusty; and then the dump lamp-post was just in front of them.

'All on the left,' Chris shouted and again they flung themselves on the left handle.

The barrow swung round and jumped across the pavement like a mad elephant and plunged into the blackness of the dump with a clatter of tins.

'Whoa, whoa,' Dusty shouted and the barrow rammed against the apple tree and overturned. There was a shrill scream and then silence. Thick black silence.

'What was that?' Dusty whispered. There was a smell of wood-smoke in the pitch black and other smells and little fluttering sounds. 'You got the matches?'

Over the wall was the towering bulk of West Flats, checked all over with lighted windows. The hair prickled on Chris's neck as he scraped the match against the box. For an instant they saw the den but it had four walls now. One wall was a dark blanket. Then the match went out.

A shout came out of the darkness and a dog barked. The boys left the barrow and ran clattering across the tins and stumbled on to the pavement. They stood under

the lamp-post staring at each other, eyes black in dead white faces.

'What is it?' Dusty whispered.

'There's kids,' Chris whispered. 'There's kids asleep in our house.'

'They got a blinkin' cheek,' said Tom.

June came running down Kings' Street as fast as she could with the old dog waddling and puffing on his lead.

'Told you,' she shouted, and her eyes were all bright with excitement. June and Chris are twins.

'Told us what?' said Chris.

'There's Gypsies on the dump,' said June. 'They came this afternoon. There's a green lorry and a big blue caravan and lots of kids and they made a fire.'

'Gypsies?' said Chris.

'What about the barrow?' said Dusty.

2 'I want Dusty's barrow'

On Monday morning it was June woke Chris. She got up and put on the light and grabbed her clothes off the chair and dived back into bed.

June's bedclothes went up like a tent and she was grunting and squirming inside, and then she sat up with her school blouse and blue jersey already on and her face all pink.

'Christmas play today,' said June. She'd been saving milk-bottle tops for the Christmas play and now she tipped the whole jar on to her bed and began to count them. Silver stars from milk-bottle tops was her own idea.

Chris lay warm under the eiderdown. It was dark outside and the windows were all cobwebbed with white frost, and there were Gypsies on the dump. What was it like to be a Gypsy?

The smell of bacon came drifting up the stairs and Mum was calling for the second time. 'Are you two getting up or aren't you? You'll be late for school.'

Chris was out of bed like a whip-lash and into his vest and shirt and jersey and trousers. It was still dark but he could see the long blue caravan by the light of the street-lamp on the pavement. It had curtains drawn at all the windows, and the top was covered with white frost like icing sugar sprinkled on a cake. Chris shivered. What was it like sleeping on the dump with a white frost?

A flickering light went on inside the caravan and the red curtains glowed like poppies. Then a boy came out; he was a bit older than Chris, twelve or thirteen perhaps. He wore ragged jeans and boots and an old coat that was too big for him, so the sleeves covered his hands.

He had a cowboy hat, black with a big brim and a long white fringe at the edge that swayed as he walked. Chris's eyes were bright with admiration. Fancy having the nerve to wear a hat like that, he thought.

The Gypsy boy knelt by the patch of last night's fire and lit some crumpled paper and blew gently. A thin coil of blue smoke rose from the sticks, and the boy sat back on his heels. Chris saw his face for the first time, a narrow, brown face with a tangle of hair and quick black eyes that swept across the backs of the houses. Could the Gypsy boy see him, Chris wondered. He waved, but the boy looked abruptly away and spat on the ground.

Liberty Lovell stared at the blob of his spittle. What they think he was, blinkin' Punch and Judy or something? There was Gaujé houses all round and Gaujé eyes watching. It made Ma tetchy as a cornered cat, and Ma was tetchy anyway with the baby coming and the wagon broke.

Either you were Gypsy or you were Gaujé and the Lovells were Gypsy. The Gaujé made the laws and the Gaujé had eyes like pebbles.

Liberty fetched the great black hook from under the wagon and hung the kettle over the fire. What were they going to do? They were hungry and it was all the Gaujé's fault. The ground was cold as iron and they had a good gas-stove in the wagon but no money for the bottle-gas and

that was the Gaujé's fault too. The money was gone on the three old cars; Pa got them cheap, a real bargain. The three cars were a fine bit of scrap and a right old party they had that night, with singing round the fire and dancing, and three chickens in the pot and Ma screeching like a jay-bird with the good luck of it.

Only the police, the 'gavvers', came next morning before there was time to break the cars and sell the scrap. Tractors towed the Gypsies off and the old wagon's back broke, brittle as bird bones, and the wheel came off and the Lovells had to leave her at the roadside. They had to leave the three cars too. Bad luck was come and the money was gone and nothing for food and it was all the Gaujé's fault.

Liberty blew on his frozen hands and the kettle began to hum like bees in clover.

Chris plunged down the stairs and crashed into Dad's bike that stood just inside the front door, like he did most mornings. Dad called out, 'Why don't you look where you're going?', like he did most mornings.

It was warm in the kitchen with the flowery curtains still drawn and the bacon sizzling in the pan, and Chris sat down at the table.

'About time too,' Mum said, and put his egg and bacon in front of him. Dad had the newspaper by the fire and his third cup of tea on the table beside him. Rags put his head on Dad's knee and Dad gave him a bit of bacon rind.

'Poor old dog, how's he going to go outside this weather?'

'You think the world of that dog,' said Mum.

'Go fur, hasn't he?' said Chris. 'Got a good coat.' He glanced sideways at Dad. Did Dad know there were Gypsies on the dump? You couldn't see the dump from the kitchen because of the yard and the high wall. Rags had a good fur coat and that was more than the Gypsy boy.

June had the jar of milk-bottle tops on the table in front of her. 'A hundred and twenty-seven silver stars,' June said. 'A skyful of stars for the Christmas play. We're starting today and doing it Thursday with everybody coming. Important people coming, Miss Lee says.'

'What about us?' Dad said, getting ready to go to work. 'We don't matter, I suppose?'

'Our tickets are on the dresser,' Mum said.

Chris wound his scarf twice round his neck. Going outside was like cold water flung in your face. People were hurrying along the High Street with blue lips and tight Monday-morning faces. June said, 'I got to get Dickie, and you got to get the barrow.'

'All right, all right,' Chris said. He didn't call for Tom; Tom's mum didn't like people calling. June ran on. Dickie was in the Infants and June always fetched him for school. Chris got farther down inside his duffle coat. Thames'd freeze up again this rate, he thought.

Dusty came out of the corner shop. 'My ears are going to drop off,' Chris said, and Dusty flicked his spectacles up his nose and said, 'What about the barrow then?'

They walked down Kings' Street towards the dump. There was a queue of people shivering at the bus stop.

'Here we are,' Chris said, and his words made white mist in the cold air. There was a smell of wood smoke as they went between the boarded-up shops. Chris stopped suddenly.

'Aren't you coming?' whispered Dusty, and his round white face went red.

'Not my auntie's barrow is it?' whispered Chris, and there was a strange smell, peppery, and the back of his neck prickled. 'Two people going is nosey. How'd you like it? Two people poking round your garden?'

'But it's not *their* garden,' whispered Dusty. 'It's *our*

dump isn't it?' June was coming down the road with the jar of bottle tops and Dickie bobbing up and down at the end of her arm like a yoyo.

'What you scared of then?' June said.

'Who says I'm scared?' whispered Dusty.

'I do,' said June, and her eyes were bright as brown buttons. 'Scaredy-cat. Scaredy-cat.'

'You shut your gob,' Chris said angrily.

'It's Gypsies,' Dickie said.

'I'll get your barrow for you,' June said, and she walked on to the dump with the jar of bottle tops in her hand. She smiled and kept on smiling because the boys were watching her, but there was this strange smell, and her heart was thumping. She walked right round the caravan. There was the den under the apple tree and the pile of wood, but there was no sign of the barrow.

On the pavement the boys were statue-still, watching her. June knocked at the caravan door. The door opened a crack and a woman's voice said, wheedling and sing-song, 'What you want then, dearie?'

'Please . . . please . . .' said June, and the door opened wider and the pepper smell was stronger, and the woman was yellowish and very thin and there were deep hollows round her black eyes and black-grey plaits looped over her ears. She had a shawl across her chest but her body was bulky and round-bellied.

'I want Dusty's barrow,' June said breathily, and the woman clutched her with a brown hand.

'Dusty Barrow? Nobody of that name 'ere.' Her voice was suddenly harsh as crows and her black eyes burned.

'Dusty's barrow?' June gasped, stepping back, and a dog leapt from under the caravan, jumping and snarling frantically at the end of its rope.

'You get off of 'ere, you,' the woman screeched.

'You let go my sister,' yelled Chris. The jar of bottle tops crashed to the ground and June turned and ran back to the pavement.

'Gypsies take you away. Gypsies take you away,' sobbed Dickie.

'Stop that,' June said, blotting his eyes with his red pixie hood.

'Where's the barrow?' Dusty said anxiously.

'Wasn't there,' said June.

'Did you hear me shout?' Chris said. 'She let go when I shouted.'

'I lost my stars,' said June, blinking hard. 'A hundred and twenty-seven silver stars.'

Chris was ashamed because he'd let June go by herself, and angry too, and he picked up a stone and flung it at the caravan. There was a crash and the tinkle of splattered glass and a long wail like the howl of a wolf.

'Got the window, didn't I?'

'Smashing shot,' Dusty said, and they grabbed Dickie and ran down Kings' Street. They didn't stop till they got to Wood Lane Primary School. 'Gypsies take you away,' Dickie whimpered, and June crouched down and put her arm round him. 'Nobody's going to take you away. Gypsies got enough kids of their own.'

The school bell clanged and they went through the gate and across the frosted playground, and June said, 'What's your auntie going to do without her barrow?'

'Going to do her nut,' said Dusty gloomily. 'They got a blinkin' cheek coming round our dump and burning up our wood.'

'I shouldn't have chucked that stone,' muttered Chris.

'Wasn't your fault,' said Dusty. 'It was her grabbing June, that big fat pig.'

'Going to have a baby wasn't she?' said June.

'A baby,' said Chris.

'Might be born Christmas,' June said, as if she knew all about it. Chris stared at her and his face went white. A baby coming and frost everywhere and snow on the forecast.

'And I broke their blinkin' window,' said Chris.

3 'Can I be Mary?'

Liberty Lovell was hungry; they all were. Pa and Ma had gone after the old wagon with its back broke and the wheel come off. The Gaujé broke your wagon and the Gaujé broke your windows; a Gypsy had to look out for himself.

Liberty walked down Wood Lane past the Gaujo school. Grey stone and grey yard and high iron railings; you didn't catch him going near a Gaujo school. 'Hairs growing on a diamond first.' Then he heard the singing: *All things bright and beautiful*. The music drew him like a magnet and he gripped the railings in his hands. Through the window he could see a great fir tree. Liberty stared. What did they want to do that for? Cut a tree from the forest and shut it up inside the school?

The Gaujé were mad as magpies. The Gaujé broke your windows.

There was a notice on the railings with black and gold letters: WOOD LANE PRIMARY SCHOOL. Liberty stared at the Gaujo writing. There were four words and Liberty frowned. 'No Gypsies served here', is that what it said?

A milk-float swished to the kerb and the milkman came round.

'Cold enough for you?' he said cheerily and then he looked at Liberty again. 'You don't want to hang about here, son,' he said as he heaved the rack of bottles off the float. 'Find yourself in trouble, you will. Off you go.'

Liberty went on down the road in his cowboy hat. His sisters were making Christmas flowers back in the wagon and Liberty had to get the twigs.

In the school hall they were singing. *Each little bud that opens*. June's mouth sang the words but her eyes were on the Christmas tree. It was bigger than last year; it stretched all green and furry up to the glass roof and its top was bent over. Friday was the Christmas party. Thursday was the Christmas play and June sighed because of the hundred and twenty-seven silver stars lost on the dump.

Linda, June's friend, was looking at the tree too.

'We'll all get presents, Friday,' she whispered.

'Hush,' whispered Mary, who wanted to be Mary in the Christmas play. 'Hush.'

'What did you get last year?' whispered June, and then her mouth sang *He made their tiny wings.*

'I forget,' said Linda. 'Something plastic. Swopped it with Rosie, didn't I?'

'You shouldn't talk in prayers,' whispered Mary, looking prim and good.

'Hark at teacher's pet,' said Linda, and she peered along the line at Miss Lee in her plum-coloured cardigan.

Mr Page, the headmaster, read the lesson and Chris wished he hadn't thrown that stone. It was the Gypsy woman grabbing June like that, Chris thought. People were funny with babies coming. Rosie's Mum ate nothing but sardines for a week before their Billy was born. Fancy living in a caravan and people throwing stones and breaking your windows when you had a baby coming. Again and again Chris heard the Gypsy woman's wail and the splinter of glass.

'What'm I going to do about my auntie's barrow?' Dusty whispered, nudging Chris.

'I dunno,' said Chris. What was *he* going to do about the broken window?

A few moments later they were hurtling up the stone stairs to the classroom. In Class Six there were three groups: 'Greens' and 'Reds' and 'Blues'. It was the 'Greens' doing the big parts in the Christmas play this year, because the 'Reds' did them last year. Chris and June and Dusty and Tom and Mary and Linda Jones and her cousin Ron, and Rosie were all 'Greens'.

Class Six was Miss Lee's class. Miss Lee tweaked her

plum-coloured cardigan and said, 'Absolute quiet. I want absolute quiet, Class Six.'

'Please, Miss . . . please, Miss, aren't we going to start our Christmas play?' said Tom bobbing up and down.

'Please can I be Mary?' said Mary, waving both hands in the air.

'She ought to be *Mary* because she is *Mary*,' said Tom.

'It's not fair. She was Mary year before, year before last,' Linda said, pouting.

'Did I say "absolute quiet" or didn't I?' said Miss Lee sharply, and everybody got their sum books out and Tom muttered, 'Always in a bad mood, Mondays.'

'It's her chilblains itching,' whispered Ron.

Miss Lee rubbed her swollen fingers. Monday was not her day. They turned the heating off at the weekend and the school was cold, and then there was dinner money, and today there was this new student teacher expected, and the Christmas play to get started, and as soon as she looked up, there were hands waving in the air like the tentacles of an octopus.

'Get on with your work, please,' said Miss Lee and the hands went slowly down.

Chris looked out of the window. The sky had a yellowish tinge and that meant snow.

On the wall beside his desk there was a picture of a village in Africa. A black man had come to Wood Lane School last term and told them about it. Everybody was very poor and lived in houses made of straw that fell down in a storm. At Wood Lane School they were very sorry and June started the blanket. She got everybody knitting squares in different colours and then she sewed them together; only people forgot their squares and the blanket was never finished. There was half a blanket in the cupboard still.

But in Africa, if your house fell down at least you had the sunshine, Chris thought. In England there was snow and people threw stones. Wasn't it worse to be a Gypsy in England?

'Please, Miss . . . they got my auntie's barrow,' Dusty stammered going pink. 'She can't do anything down the market without her barrow.'

'Who's got your auntie's barrow?' said Miss Lee.

'Gypsies,' muttered Dusty, and again hands were waving all round the classroom.

'Please, Miss . . . there's Gypsies on the dump,' said Tom. 'Big 'uns and little 'uns. They came last night.'

'They got my auntie's barrow,' said Dusty.

'You mean the Gypsies have taken your auntie's barrow?' said Miss Lee.

'Course they have,' Tom jumped up excitedly. 'We'll go round after school, all the lot of us.'

'Takes more'n a tribe of Gypsies to scare us,' said Ron.

'Blinkin' Gypsies, not their dump is it?' said Linda and her cheeks went red.

'Not your dump either,' muttered Chris.

'Our mum says we don't want dirty Gypsies living next to us,' said Linda. 'Can't even read, Gypsies can't.'

'Gypsy children don't get the chance of going to school and learning to read because they're moving all the time,' Miss Lee said.

'Lucky duckers,' muttered Ron.

'Anyroad they won't be on the dump long,' said Tom knowingly, and everybody looked at him. 'My mum's got this letter saying we don't want Gypsies on the dump. She's getting everybody to sign it.' Miss Lee pursed her lips because Tom's mum was always writing letters to Miss Lee, complaining letters mostly.

'Your mum would,' Chris muttered.

'What's that?' Tom said glaring angrily, because Chris was his friend and ought to be on his side.

'I'm not signing any rotten letter,' Chris said. 'Gypsies got to go somewhere, haven't they?'

'She's not asking you to sign, stupid,' said Tom scornfully. 'Gypsies on the dump's got nothing to do with kids.'

'Well, it's our dump, isn't it?' said June.

Miss Lee rubbed her chilblains irritably; half-past two and still the student teacher hadn't come.

'We'll start our play now,' she said, going to the big cupboard, and everyone came buzzing over like wasps round a honey pot.

'Where's the books?' said Linda as the cupboard creaked open.

'There's the bit of blanket we made for the Africans,' said Chris grabbing hold of it.

'Wait a minute, wait a minute,' said Miss Lee.

'Please ... can I be Mary?' said Mary, and she grabbed the blue curtain that was always Mary's blue robe.

'It's not fair,' said Linda and she grabbed it too, and Chris was pulling at the African blanket and everything fell out of the cupboard just as the door opened.

'Er . . . this is Mr Beach,' said Mr Page.

Mr Beach was tall and thin with very long legs and orange fair hair that stuck out round his head like a double marigold. He had a yellow shirt and a yellow tie that matched and orange corduroy trousers.

'Coo, smashing,' whispered Linda, still holding on to the blue Mary robe.

'Dishy dresser,' whispered Chris.

'Dishy dish,' whispered Linda, and June went rather pink.

'Smashing cords,' whispered Dusty flicking his spectacles up his nose. 'I'm getting cords for Christmas.'

Mr Beach was a drama student, and drama was plays, Mr Page said, and Mr Beach was going to do the Christmas play this year because Miss Lee had done it every year for ever so long and she deserved a rest. Miss Lee pursed her lips and said, 'Thank you, Mr Page.' But Class Six knew she wasn't pleased. So did Mr Beach.

Everybody was shouting and crowding round him in his yellow shirt.

'Where can we go for rehearsal?' said Mr Beach.

The cloakroom was the only quiet place and a moment later the 'Greens' were hurtling down the stone stairs. It was rather dark and smelt of disinfectant and gumboots. Mr Beach had a record-player under his arm and he went down the stairs three at a time. 'He's like a blinkin' daddy-long-legs,' said Dusty.

'You shut up,' said June.

Everyone was pushing in and out of the coats, hanging on the pegs and trying on things from the cupboard. Chris draped the African blanket round his shoulders. Be great for Joseph, he thought.

June was explaining to Mr Beach about the lost silver stars and her face was pink.

'Please, sir, can I be Mary?' said Mary with a very sweet smile and the blue curtain draped over her head.

'She was Mary year before, year before last,' said Linda, pouting.

'We forgot the books,' said Rosie.

'We don't want books,' said Mr Beach.

'Course we don't, I know Mary's part by heart,' said Mary.

'Shut up, will you?' said Mr Beach, and his marigold hair

fell over his eyes as he fixed the plug on the record-player.

'Fancy a teacher saying "shut up". I'm telling my mum,' whispered Mary with her blue eyes very round.

'Shut up and sit down,' said Mr Beach. 'Forget all that stuff about stars and blue robes. Just listen to this music and think of a man and a woman. They're very poor and the woman has a baby coming and they have nowhere to go. Shut your eyes and listen.'

Everybody shut their eyes and the music started. Nobody had heard music like it before; it was Eastern music. It went up and down like somebody wailing. Chris opened his eyes with a start. It was like the wailing cry of the Gypsy woman and she had a baby coming too and she was poor . . .

The music was very loud and Dusty slipped between the pegs and went across to the window; he hated plays and everybody looking at him.

Outside a few flakes of snow floated in the grey air, and beyond the railings two Gypsy children were dancing to the music. It was Liberty and his sister, Pattella. Then Dusty saw the barrow piled up with holly.

'They got Auntie's barrow,' he shouted.

4 A barrow of holly

Liberty heard the Gaujé children, and then they were streaming out across the snow-specked playground, scarves flying and satchels bumping.

'Come on then,' Liberty shouted to his sister. He grabbed the barrow of holly and ran off down Wood Lane. A chase was a chase any time. Took more'n a Gaujo to catch a Gypsy fox. The snow in their faces was like icy little tongues.

'After 'em,' shouted Chris as the Gypsies disappeared round the corner into Kings' Street. 'Get Dusty's barrow.'

'Stop thief,' shouted Tom and then everybody was racing down the pavement yelling, 'Stop thief. Stop thief.'

'Don't let 'em get back to the dump,' shouted Dusty.

In Kings' Street the evening rush was just beginning and the pavement was crowded. Pattella was in front and Liberty looked back over his shoulder. The Gaujé kids were already at the corner. He'd seen hounds get a fox once, a big dog-fox with thick red fur and the hounds baying and running, pink tongues and sharp white teeth. Liberty's heart lurched in his chest; like a muddy old rag, that dead fox.

'Stop thief.'

It was Tom grabbed Liberty. There was a ripping sound, and Pattella shrieked like a trapped hare. Liberty's sleeve came away all white and ragged at the shoulder and he let go the barrow and flung his back against the boarded-up shops; the cowboy hat went spinning across the pavement.

'Get out of it, you,' he shouted desperately.

The barrow lurched across the pavement with Pattella clinging to one handle. The bus queue jumped back as it thudded against the bus stop and tipped sideways into the gutter. Holly spilled across the road and four buns slid from a paper bag, white and round against the greasy black. Pattella sat down on the edge of the pavement, pulled her ragged red cardigan over her head and wailed loudly.

'What a shame,' said the lady in the front of the bus queue. She had a big fur coat all polka-dotted with snow and a shopping basket on wheels. 'Why can't you leave the poor Gypsy children alone?'

'I like that,' said Tom, breathless and indignant. 'They took Dusty's barrow didn't they? Didn't they take your barrow?'

'It's not my barrow, it's Auntie's barrow,' Dusty muttered, going pink because everybody was looking at him and Pattella was crying. Rosie started crying too.

'You're a thief,' said Tom, turning back to Liberty.

'Never took nothing. Left the old barrow didn't 'ee?' Liberty muttered. 'Look what 'ee done. Only coat us got.' He pulled at the torn shoulder and his dark eyes filled with tears. A Gypsy had to think quick and Liberty was hungry. Pattella howled loudly, her thin shoulders shook under her red cardigan.

'It's disgraceful,' the lady at the front of the queue said. 'I've a good mind to call a policeman.'

Pattella's howling stopped abruptly. A policeman was always bad luck for a Gypsy. She moaned softly, twisting her fingers into the tangled black of her hair.

'Look at the poor child's hands,' cried the lady. 'They're all red and raw.'

Chris stared. Was it blood on her hands? You could cut yourself badly with broken glass.

'But it *was* Dusty's barrow,' June tried to explain.

'It's your barrow isn't it, Dusty?' said Tom.

'Not mine exactly . . .' Dusty stammered and he grabbed the barrow and trundled it away down the wet black road.

'Young hooligans, that's what you are,' the lady said.

Chris picked up the cowboy hat and gave it to Liberty. He tried to smile but he didn't feel like smiling. It was the worst day of his life: the broken window and Pattella's hands, and the holly all tipped up, and Tom's mum and everybody wanting the Gypsies off the dump.

'Sorry,' said Chris.

'I should think so too,' said the lady, and Pattella's hand waved in the air like a small pink flag.

'Poor little thing,' the lady said and she put five pence into Pattella's palm.

'You ought to get something for those hands,' she said to Liberty.

'Get her round the chemist soon as us got the money,' said Liberty, saluting so that the white fringe swung on his hat. The lady put another five pence in Pattella's hand.

'He's got a nerve,' said Tom.

'Yes,' said Chris admiringly. What was he going to do?

'There's our bus,' said the man, relieved.

'Bless 'ee, lady,' said Liberty, springing forward and holding out his hat. 'Bless you too, Guvnor. Bless your kind 'eart.'

'Well . . .' The man dropped a ten-penny piece into Liberty's hat.

'Something for 'er poor hands. Something for 'er supper.'

Liberty chanted as the bus queue moved into the bus.

'I like that,' said Tom indignantly as the bus pulled away and Liberty counted the money he'd collected. 'He gets paid for pinching people's barrows.'

'He only borrowed it,' said Chris. Pattella sat up; her eyes were black as beetles. She had gold ear-rings, and two front teeth missing. Liberty looked at the sky; already it was tinged with dark-time blue. 'Smell the snow coming and us got nothing to eat,' he said mournfully.

'Like a lemon sherbet, would you?' said Chris, pulling the bag out of his pocket. They'd all got warm kitchens to go to and cooked teas and it wasn't fair.

'Didn't finish my sandwiches dinner-time,' Rosie said, looking in her satchel, and Pattella grabbed the sandwich and stuffed it in her mouth.

'She'll choke herself,' Tom said.

'Must be awful to be hungry,' said Rosie sniffing. Any thing sad made Rosie cry; she had to go out once when Miss Lee read *The Little Tin Soldier*.

'Got real gold ear-rings, hasn't she?' Mary said, and Pattella grinned with pride. 'Her mum could sell her ear-rings and get food, couldn't she?'

A new queue formed at the bus stop. Liberty watched it under the brim of his hat.

'Look what 'ee done to Liberty's coat,' he moaned, and Pattella began to cry again with her mouth full of sandwich. The bus queue stared at them stonily.

'What we going to do now?' June said, looking at Chris.

'Holly's all right,' Chris said, and he jumped forward and gathered an armful off the road. 'First thing is to get this round the dump.'

It was almost dark on the dump and thick with wood-smoke and the caravan windows glowed like red eyes.

There was brown paper stuck on the broken pane.

'Where's your mum?' whispered June nervously.

'Gone,' said Liberty, and the lorry was gone too. Pattella followed the others, wailing loudly.

'Shut your mouth and get inside, you,' Liberty said and Pattella stopped and went into the wagon. Chris gazed at Liberty. That was the way to talk to your sister all right. He glanced at June, and June put out her tongue.

Liberty threw more wood on the fire and red sparks rose into the darkness. 'That's our wood,' said Tom, and Liberty scowled. 'Everything's Gaujo.'

'We fetched it from the old airfield,' said Chris. 'Dusty and me and Tom, but you can have it and welcome.'

'What are we going to do now?' said June.

It was bitter cold and Dusty and Linda and Mary and Ron had gone home for tea.

'Sell the holly, aren't we?' Chris said.

'Can't sell holly dark-time,' Liberty said.

'Course we can't,' said Tom.

'Course we can,' said Chris, and his voice bubbled with nis great idea; it would cancel out the broken window. 'We could knock on doors because everybody knows us, see? There's an old pram round here somewhere.' Chris moved off into the darkness.

'There's our Billy's pram in the shed at home,' whispered Rosie.

'Get it then,' said Tom. Chris was his friend and Chris's ideas were catching, and it was Tom's mum wanted to get the Gypsies off, not Tom, and Billy's pram was a smart white pram with a flower on the side. He wouldn't mind pushing that down the High Street.

'I bags Rosie's pram,' said Tom as Chris came clattering out of the darkness with the old black pram.

'What about your mum and her letter?' Chris said.

'Going to tear it up, aren't I?' said Tom.

'You really?' said Chris.

'Course I am,' said Tom.

'You'll catch it,' said June admiringly.

The Gaujé kids had gone and Liberty slipped into the wagon and shut the door quickly against the cold dark-time air. It was hot from the old Queenie stove which burned wood. His five small sisters stared at him from the table which was covered with wood-shavings and bottles of red ink. Pattella's knife went slowly down the white stick, peeling petals that curled back like chrysanthemums. When the flower was finished she dipped it in the ink. Her fingers were quick as lizards. They were all quick-fingered, even little Minta, and their hands were all stained with red ink.

'Gaujé kids selling us holly,' Liberty grinned. Only fools and horses worked.

'Gaujé kids can't sell nothing,' said Pattella scornfully.

'Minta's hungry,' whimpered the little girl. ' 'Er's dark-time and Minta . . .'

There was a knock at the wagon door and instantly the Gypsy children were silent.

'Gavvers?' breathed Pattella and Liberty froze. Pa and Ma gone for the old wagon and him looking out for the little 'uns and the gavvers come. He twitched the edge of the curtain and peered through the black crack.

'Can't see nothing,' he whispered. Another knock vibrated through the wagon and June's voice said, 'Liberty Lovell?'

Liberty opened the door and his black eyes stared down under the white fringe of his hat. 'What you want, you?'

'Got you a loaf,' said June, holding it out. 'Couldn't get buns.' Liberty watched as she ran off across the dump, her white socks flicking like a rabbit's scut in the darkness.

Then he put the loaf in the middle of the table. A moment later nothing but the waxy paper was left. The Lovells were hungry.

'We'll go down to the big houses,' said Tom as he and Rosie pushed the white pram down Wood Lane. He didn't want to see anybody he knew. If somebody told his mum he was out selling holly in a pram he'd never hear the end of it.

'Isn't half cold,' said Rosie, and as they passed Wood Lane School the street-lamp shining through the railings made dark tiger-stripes across the playground.

'What about West Flats?' said Rosie.

'Too many stairs,' said Tom because his mum had friends

in West Flats, and they went on past the great block and down the road. Tom stopped outside a house with a low wall and shrubs and a tiled path to the front door.

'You're never going in there?' whispered Rosie.

'Course I am,' said Tom. He pushed the pram up the garden path. The door bell chimed like a peal of bells and Rosie slipped back into the darkness.

'What you blinkin' scared of?' Tom whispered, and then there were footsteps and a dark shadow in the glass of the door and a lady opened it.

'Like a nice bunch of Christmas holly for five pence?' Tom said loud and jaunty, so Rosie'd hear he wasn't scared.

'Wait a moment,' the lady said crisply. 'Just wait there.'

Tom stood on the doorstep; suddenly he felt nervous. 'Rosie,' he whispered, peering into the darkness, but Rosie was running back up Wood Lane as fast as she could.

A man came to the door with a torch in his hand.

'I've got something to show you,' he said in a gruff voice.

'What?' said Tom, and his heart jumped unpleasantly as the man gripped his arm and led him down the path. The torch-light hovered over something stark and white among the shrubs. It was a hacked and twisted stump with a few holly twigs sticking out at the bottom.

'Ten years ago I put that holly in,' said the man. He spoke quietly but his voice trembled. 'Never had a berry on it, not till this year. Know what happened this afternoon? My wife went out shopping, and when she got back it was gone, hacked off.'

Suddenly the torch was shining right in his eyes and Tom blinked and stammered. 'But I didn't, I was at school.'

'Don't bother to explain to me,' the man said, holding Tom firmly. 'My wife has already phoned the police.'

5 A bucket of water

Chris and June hurried along the High Street. They had to drag the old black pram like a sledge because two of the wheels were rusted up. The Town Hall clock struck six in the chill navy-blue sky.

They'd been shy, at first, selling the holly, starting off with Dickie's mum and then going next door to Dickie's mum's friend. After that they'd gone right down the High Street and not cared for anyone, and now thirty pence rattled in Chris's pocket. Thirty pence for Liberty in his cowboy hat, that was really something.

'Let's try the corner shop,' said June. Mr Miller kept open long after the Co-op and all the other shops were closed. It was warm inside the corner shop and Mrs Jones, Linda's mum, was there.

'Like to buy some holly?' Chris said, and Mr Miller in his white coat said, 'Serving Mrs Jones, aren't I?' The ham slicer swung back and forth and petals of pink ham curled on to the paper. 'Lived here twenty years and never anything like this,' Mrs Jones was saying. 'My clean wash all covered with black bits from their filthy fire.'

Mr Miller clucked sympathetically and rang open the till. 'That's twenty-two pence, Mrs Jones.'

'Never had Gypsies for neighbours and I'm not going to start now,' said Mrs Jones with a sour glance at Chris and June and the battered black pram. 'Used to be a nice neighbourhood round here.'

'Mrs White's going round the Council with her letter first thing. That should shift them,' Mr Miller said, and Chris looked at June and winked. Not if Tom got hold of it.

'Sooner the better,' said Mrs Jones and the shop bell clanged behind her, and Mr Miller walked across and put up the latch.

'What you want to bring that old pram in here for? She'll be round the Co-op next week,' he said.

'Sorry, Mr Miller,' Chris said. 'Like to buy a nice bit of holly?'

'They're putting Christmas trees in the Co-op window,' June said.

'How much?' Mr Miller said opening the till.

'Only thirty pence for all this lot,' said Chris, stacking the holly on the bacon counter. 'This week's special offer.'

'Cheeky monkey,' said Mr Miller.

They parked the empty pram outside number twenty-five. Nobody would see it because Tom's mum never let anybody use her front room.

'We'll take the money round the dump after tea,' Chris whispered as they slipped into the warm passage of their own house.

'Mum'll never let us, night like this,' June whispered, and Rags came out, his long nails clanking on the lino.

'Where you two get to then?' Mum called from the kitchen.

'Got a new teacher, Mr Beach,' June said, hanging her coat on the peg.

'Can't he tell the time?' said Mum, and Chris crept upstairs. The Gypsy's fire glowed red in the darkness. Had Mrs White been round to Mum with the letter? Perhaps Mum didn't even know the Gypsies were there?

In the kitchen Mum lifted the chip basket from the pan,

hot fat fell in golden drops and June said, 'He's smashing, our new teacher. I'm going to be a teacher when I grow up. He's got a yellow shirt and a yellow tie that matches and he says the Christmas play's got to come out of our heads and not out of any book.'

'They all got their own ideas,' Mum said, putting plates of sausages and chips on the table. 'Mrs White was round the school half-past four. Saw your new teacher with his yellow shirt and his long hair, didn't she?'

'It's not long,' said June going pink. 'It's lovely.'

There was a blast of cold air as Dad wheeled his bicycle into the passage.

'What's going on at number twenty-five?' Dad said, clicking off his trouser clips. 'There's a policeman on the doorstep and two prams stuck outside. Been doing a bit of shop-lifting, has she?'

'Don't be daft,' said Mum.

'What policeman?' said Chris huskily. Had Mrs White been to the police about the Gypsies instead of the Town Hall?

'It'll be Sergeant Bates for Mr White,' Mum said. 'They play darts together round The Bull.'

'What's Sergeant Bates want with two prams?' Dad said, and just then Chris got a coughing fit.

'Serves you right for talking with your mouth full,' Mum said. 'I wasn't,' Chris gasped with his eyes watering.

Tea was over and they'd got to get out again somehow.

'Old dog wants a walk,' said Chris going out into the passage.

'No, he doesn't,' Dad said, and June lifted Rags's brown velvet ear and whispered, 'Lovely walk, lovely walk.' Rags thumped his tail and stayed where he was. June had to wait until Dad got up to fiddle with the telly, then she bundled Rags out of the kitchen. 'Lovely walk, lovely walk,' she whispered, but Rags sat down in the cold passage, so she had to slide him down the lino to Chris.

'Get his lead on, quick,' she whispered, grabbing her coat, and Mum called from the scullery, 'Where d'you think you're going this time of night?'

'Old dog wants a walk,' shouted Chris, and they shot out on to the pavement and slammed the front door behind them. 'Thames'll freeze this rate,' said Chris, and his breath was white in the darkness and Rags sat down on the pavement and whined. 'You'll have to tighten his collar,' June said, and Chris struggled with the cold brass buckle.

'Let's put him in the pram,' he whispered, and he carried Rags to number twenty-five.

'What's Dad mean about *two* prams?' June said.

'Seeing double,' Chris said. 'Perhaps he dropped into The Bull on his way home.'

'Hope Tom's all right,' said June.

They pushed the pram round to the dump, and Chris knocked at the caravan door this time, and Liberty opened it a narrow crack.

'Got the holly money for you,' Chris said.

Liberty opened the door wider and said, 'Get in then.'

'Your ma got back yet?' whispered June anxiously.

'Naw,' said Liberty; he was still wearing his cowboy hat. 'Won't be back this dark-time, 'er won't.'

'All right then,' said Chris. 'Just for a minute.'

They stood blinking in the warm stuffiness and the strange smell, and Chris unwound his scarf and rubbed his freezing ears. The five little girls turned round from the Christmas flowers at the table and stared at the Gaujé children with prune black eyes.

'What you making?' June said, staring at their red-stained hands. Something for 'er poor hands, Liberty had said to the bus queue, but it was only red ink. June frowned.

'Christmas flowers, ain't 'er?' Liberty answered, and Pattella screeched, 'What yer want to let the Gaujé come in 'ere for? Bad luck lettin' Gaujé in the wagon.'

'You shut your mouth, you,' Liberty scowled. 'Us don't want 'em standing at the door and the gavvers see the light?' And besides that Liberty wanted the Gaujé kids to see what the Gypsies got. Standing there with their pale eyes popping out on stalks, and no wonder with the red shade on the lamp and red curtains and leopard pattern seats with red cushions and red paper flowers in vases on the walls, Liberty thought. There was a glass cupboard at the end with red and gold cups, set out for beauty and never used, and a silver bicycle bell, and best of all a crystal door knob, bright as any diamond. What the Gaujé got better'n that? Liberty smiled to himself as June looked round the wagon and her mouth went round as a coin.

'Got your eyes full,' said Pattella sharply. 'Our place, ain't 'er?'

'I'm only looking,' June said. 'And you stopped on the dump and the dump is *our* place.'

'Gaujé got every blinkin' place,' said Liberty, and little Minta began to cry. 'Gaujé going to put us off?'

'Course they're not,' said Chris. 'Stay here as long as you like. The dump is *our* place and that's our den because we made it but you can have it and all the wood . . .' Then he remembered Mrs White with her letter and Mrs Jones in the corner shop and her washing spoilt and all the other people round the dump who wanted to get the Gypsies off. 'Well here's your money anyway,' he said miserably. He put it on the table and Liberty left it where it was, silver and brown in the wood shavings.

'Gavvers broke us old wagon,' Pattella said fiercely. 'Police broke the old wagon's back.'

'The police don't break things,' June said.

'They don't break Gaujé things,' said Liberty, and he thought of Ma screaming mad and the baby soon and the cars left by the road and he sighed. 'Us Gypsies got nowhere to stop.'

'Why don't you go out to the fields?' said June.

'Summertime us work in the fields, pickin' and that, and the Gaujé let us stop,' said Liberty. 'Wintertime ain't no work and 'er don't let us stop. Us got nowhere to stop.'

'It's not fair. You got to stop somewhere,' said June.

'Why don't you just stop here?' said Chris. 'There's lots of wood and only the one way in. Make a big barricade then the police can't get in and they'll have to let you stop.' Chris's eyes were bright as two candles.

'Can't,' said Liberty. 'Ain't got no water.'

'Give us your bucket then,' said Chris. He had broken their window, but he'd made up for it, hadn't he? Selling their holly for them and getting water? He was their friend now, Liberty's friend.

Number twenty-one. Chris opened the door quietly. Sounds of gunfire came from the kitchen. Mum and Dad liked a good cowboy film on the telly. Chris crept out to the scullery, no sense disturbing them, but before he could turn the tap Mum called, 'What you doing with that bucket?'

'Getting some water, aren't I?' said Chris.

'Oh no, you're not,' said Mum sharply. She didn't often get cross, not like Tom's mum, but now her cheeks were red and her mouth was all tight. 'It's those blinkin' Gypsies, isn't it? Well they're not getting water from this house.'

'But . . . what they going to do?' said Chris. 'There's six kids. They've got to have water to drink, haven't they?'

'We didn't ask them to stop on the dump, did we?' said Mum. 'You take that bucket right back . . . what's her at number twenty-five going to say if she sees you?'

'Dirty people, Gypsies,' Dad said, and suddenly Chris was angry. 'How they going to get clean without water?' he shouted, and Dad turned right round.

'Where's the old dog got to then?' he said, and Chris went pink because Rags was still sitting in the pram on the dump.

'He's round the dump,' Chris said.

'Round the dump, round the dump,' shouted Dad, and his face went as red as a peony. 'Poor old dog'll catch his death, perishing night like this.'

'Come on,' Chris whispered. June scrambled down the wall with Rags tucked under her arm; his plump body quivered like a jelly. Liberty sat astride the top. A Gypsy had no business in a Gaujo school but he had to get water somewhere. He jumped down. There were lights in several windows and the click-click of the caretaker's broom.

'What's that?' whispered Liberty.

'Chap sweeping,' whispered Chris. 'Caretaker, Mr Davis.'

Liberty stood in the doorway of the wash-block, scowling under his cowboy hat at the shining Gaujo whiteness and the bright silver taps. Water was bad luck for Gypsies, water was drowning, Ma said. He let Chris fill the bucket and the water came rushing and frothing from the tap.

'You can get a bucket every night. Only don't let Mr Davis see you,' Chris whispered, and then Rags growled and there were footsteps in the playground and suddenly Mr Beach stood in the door. Liberty got ready to run.

'What's going on? Who's this?'

'Liberty Lovell, Sir,' said Chris and June.

'Neptune Smith,' said Liberty, because a Gypsy didn't want to tell a Gaujo anything, and Mr Beach laughed and pushed back his orange fair hair.

'The Gypsies have stopped on the dump,' said June quickly. 'They got nowhere else to stop. The police towed 'em off the last place and broke their old wagon and they only got one wagon for eight people.'

'Nine,' said Liberty scowling.

'And now Mrs White and everybody's trying to get them put off the dump,' said Chris.

'But listen, the Council's supposed to make proper winter sites for the Gypsies. It's the new law,' said Mr Beach.

'Council's Gaujo, ain't 'er?' Liberty muttered, and Mr Beach frowned and looked from one to the other. There was a story here somewhere and his girl friend, Julie, was a reporter on the *Mercury*. Julie had talked about the Gypsy problem. The Gypsies were moved on and the children got no schooling so they couldn't get jobs even if they wanted because they couldn't read and write.

'You know what? You ought to come to school, Liberty Lovell Neptune Smith,' said Mr Beach.

Liberty scowled fiercely. '"Hairs growin' on a diamond first". School is for Gaujé ain't 'er?'

'Everybody should learn to write his own name,' said Mr Beach. 'Otherwise you can't get work.'

'Only fools and horses work,' Liberty shouted, angry and frightened as well. He hated this Gaujo place and its Gaujo smell, and this Gaujo man with hair stuck round his head like a dandelion, and he shouted, 'Us Gypsy writing got drowned in the sea, 'er did, and learning Gaujo writing turns us mad as magpies. Our gran told Liberty.'

'Listen, Liberty Lovell,' said Mr Beach, and his voice was low and eager. 'Your gran is an old woman and that's an old tale of hers. A Gypsy can learn to read and write like anybody else.'

'Can't,' hissed Liberty.

'Gypsy's as good as Gaujo, isn't he?' said Mr Beach and he grinned a challenge, and Liberty rubbed his sleeve across his face. 'Naw, Gypsy's better,' he said.

A car hooted twice on the dark road outside. 'That's Julie. That's for me,' said Mr Beach. 'You come to school tomorrow, Liberty Lovell, eh? And we'll try to find somewhere your people can stop. Get on to the Council.'

Liberty was gone over the wall like a cat and into the cold darkness. June and Chris followed Mr Beach out of the school gates. A small car waited by the kerb. There was a waft of scent as Julie leaned across from the driving seat. She had long fair hair and a beaded headband on her forehead.

'Hallo, Julie, listen I got a great Gypsy story for you,' Mr Beach said as he got into the car. 'You know the old dump. . . ?' The car moved off down the road and Chris and June stood on the cold pavement. Rags whined miserably.

'That's his girl friend, Julie. Smashing isn't she? Coo, lovely pong,' Chris sniffed the cold air. 'Smells like a flower shop.'

'Pet shop, more like,' snapped June. She tweaked at the lead angrily. 'Him and his silly old play. I'm glad I did drop the stars on the dump.'

'What's up with you?' Chris stared wonderingly at June. Girls were funny; there was no understanding a girl even if she was your sister.

6 Tuesday morning

In the night Chris heard the rain. It pecked at the window like sharp little beaks. In the morning it was still raining and the wheels of the blue caravan were deep in black mud.

'Look at that,' said Chris. 'The dump's all mud.'

'It's the Council ought to make a proper place for the Gypsies,' said June.

'I wish we could do something,' Chris said, and June said she was going to get everybody knitting coloured squares and finish the African blanket for the Gypsies.

After breakfast June went off to fetch Dickie, and Chris turned up the collar of his raincoat and pulled his head in like a tortoise. He couldn't see much and he walked right into the policeman standing outside number twenty-five.

'Want to look where you're going, son,' said the policeman.

'Sorry,' gasped Chris and then the door opened and the policeman stepped inside and the door slammed shut.

Dusty was waiting at the corner shop. 'What's that policeman want at number twenty-five?' said Dusty.

Chris shook his head. 'Sergeant Bates plays darts with Mr White.'

'That wasn't Sergeant Bates,' said Dusty as they turned into Kings' Street.

'What did your auntie say about the barrow?' said Chris.

'Plenty,' said Dusty gloomily.

The school Christmas tree was all silver tinsel and little lights in red and blue and green. June and Linda pressed their noses to the glass door.

'Lovely, isn't it,' Linda said.

'Your mum was on about the Gypsies in the corner shop,' June said.

'Everybody's on about the Gypsies,' Linda said, and Mary came in with a big baby doll. Chris said, 'What you want to bring that doll for?'

'Excuse me, it's baby Jesus,' Mary said.

'What did that policeman want round your house?' Chris said. 'What policeman?' Mary said, because her mum said not to talk about it.

'Did Tom tear up the letter?' Chris said, and Mary's blue eyes flickered and she went on to the cloakroom with baby Jesus tucked under her arm.

Tom was upstairs in the classroom already. The bell went for prayers but he didn't go down. *Onward Christian Soldiers* drifted up from the hall and Tom bent over his sum book. His eyes were red and puffy and the black figures jumped on the page and each one was as prickly as a holly leaf. The Whites had never had anything like it before: trouble with the police and stolen holly. Tom's mum was very angry. That's what happened if you had anything to do with Gypsies, she said. Tom was angry too. He hated Gypsies now.

Class Six came up the stairs and Chris stopped by Tom's desk. 'Did you get the letter?' he whispered. Tom bent his head low and didn't answer.

'Liberty Lovell is coming to school. You got his holly money?' Chris said, and still Tom didn't answer.

'What's up with him?' said Linda.

'Got out the wrong side the bed,' said Ron.

'Can't get out the wrong side of my bed,' said Dusty. 'It's against the wall.'

'I know what it is . . .' said Rosie.

'You shut your gob, you,' Tom hissed, and his eyes were desperate with shame.

Miss Lee took the register. 'Ron Bell.'

'Yes, Miss.'

It was always the same the end of the Christmas term, Miss Lee thought, nothing but rush, and now it was Tuesday already and only two days to Thursday and the whole play given over to Mr Beach, when she'd done it for six years and been congratulated every time, and now Mr Beach was late again.

'Mary White, Tom White.'

'Yes Miss.' Miss Lee finished the register and noticed Tom's red eyes, but a boy was best left to his troubles, Miss Lee thought, and Mary White was standing up with a large baby doll cradled in her arms.

'Please, Miss Lee, who's going to be Mary?' she said.

'She was Mary year before, year before last,' Linda whispered. 'Not fair.'

'It's up to Mr Beach now,' Miss Lee said. 'How did the rehearsal go yesterday?'

'Didn't even get started,' Mary said.

'We're not using books,' Chris explained.

'It's all coming out of our heads,' June said.

'Out of your heads?' said Miss Lee, and her eyebrows flew up towards her hair. 'Oh dear!'

Then Mr Beach came in wearing a moss green shirt and a tie that matched, and his hair was sticking out even more than usual.

'Sorry, Miss Lee, I had to see somebody at the Town Hall,' he said breathlessly. At least he'd found out what the Council was going to do about a winter site for the Gypsies.

'Shall I get the things out of the cupboard?' Linda said, and Mary grabbed the blue curtain quick as lightning, and all the 'Greens' grabbed some kind of costume and ran down the stairs to the cloakroom.

Tom followed slowly with his sum book in his hand.

'For the first scene we need Mary and Joseph and an innkeeper and a donkey,' shouted Mr Beach.

The cloakroom smelt of wet raincoats and plastic.

'Bags I'm Mary,' shouted Mary.

'Bags, I'm the donkey,' said Dusty, because the donkey was right underneath an old grey blanket. Chris pushed close to Mr Beach. 'Liberty Lovell hasn't come,' he said urgently.

'Never mind,' said Mr Beach. 'I've found out about things.'

'What things?' said Chris, and he had to shout because of the din.

'The Council's been considering a winter site for the Gypsies,' said Mr Beach. 'Wait till Julie gets hold of this.'

'We don't want Gypsies round the dump,' said Mary, with the blue curtain draped round her.

'We do,' said June. 'And Liberty's coming to this school.'

Tom looked up from his sum book and his face went dark red. 'We're not having Gypsies coming to this school,' he said.

Liberty twitched the wagon curtain and looked at the dump and the mud dotted with rusty tins and the Gaujé houses, dark grey from the rain. Inside the wagon the little girls worked at the Christmas flowers, murmuring like chickens. Water dripped in two places where the wagon roof leaked.

Liberty shivered. Where was Pa and Ma and Hopsy and the lorry and the old wagon with her back broke? Couldn't go to the Gaujo school till Ma and Pa got back.

Somebody was standing on the edge of the pavement – a policeman – and Liberty let the curtain fall and turned out the lamp and slid the bolt across the door, and crouched behind it, his heart thumping in his chest.

'Gavvers,' he whispered. The girls sat perfectly still, staring at the door with round, dark eyes.

They heard the clank of heavy boots on tins as the policeman picked his way through the mud. There was a sharp knock.

'Anybody there?'

Inside the wagon the six children were still as mice. There was a second knock but they didn't move, hardly seemed to breathe. Then there was a small rustling sound and the edge of a buff envelope poked under the door. But Liberty's hand was there, stopping the envelope coming further, so it wouldn't lodge.

'Tch,' the policeman clicked his tongue irritably. There was nowhere else he could put it. The door handle turned, and then they heard his footsteps going away across the dump.

'Come on,' said Liberty urgently.

'Where?' whispered Pattella.

'Over the Gaujo school afore the gavver comes back,' Liberty whispered.

'Gaujé going to tow us off?' little Minta whispered.

'Can't,' said Liberty, and he grinned triumphantly. 'Got to give us 'viction order first. Gavver got the eviction order but us ain't 'ad 'er.'

'Us don't want to go to school,' said Pattella.

'Us got to learn to write us name,' said Liberty.

'And Minta?' Pattella said smiling because little Minta was born daffodil time two years back, or was it three? How could Minta write her name?

'Can't leave 'er 'ere for the gavvers,' Liberty said and they jumped down and scampered across the mud.

They perched like birds along the top of the wall in ragged cardigans, red and violet and blue; two of them were barefoot and caked with mud to the ankles. The six Gypsy children stared down at the wet playground of the Gaujo school.

7 'Us come to school'

'Don't you go talking to no Gaujé kids,' Liberty said, jumping down first and lifting the little ones off the damp grey wall. The Gaujé were dirty, Ma said. Men, women and children washed in the same basin even. Pattella pulled their cardigans straight and tightened the pin that held Minta's jersey across her chest.

'Us don't talk to no Gaujé,' she said. ' "Hairs growin' on a diamond first".' The wet playground was patched with black puddles and sounds of singing came from the school, but nobody came out.

'Us oughta get in there,' whispered Pattella, pointing to the open back door. Inside, steps went down to the cloakroom. You didn't catch Liberty going in a black rabbit-hole place like that.

'Hold yer tongue, you,' Liberty scowled, glaring under the white fringe of his hat.

Chris came out. Chris was Joseph, and he had a bit of striped material tied round his head. He ran jumping over the dark puddles and Pattella called out, 'Us come.' Chris stopped dead, seeing the six Gypsy children standing by the wall.

'Us come to school,' Liberty said.

'What, all this lot?' said Chris huskily. Liberty Lovell was expected but not six Gypsy children, and some of them not even big enough for the Infants. Chris gaped, and then he shot back down the stairs.

The cloakroom roared with noise as the 'Greens' got ready for scene one. Mr Beach was playing the Eastern music and everybody was trying things on. Tom was going to be the inn-keeper. He was making the inn in one corner of the cloak-room, using benches for walls. An inn was like a pub, Tom said, they were going to have singing like at The Bull. Dusty and Ron were under the grey blanket making donkey noises.

'Gypsies,' Chris whispered to June, and Dusty heard too and stuck his head out of the blanket.

'Where?' said June.

'In the playground,' said Chris and they scampered up the stairs again, and Dusty and Mary and several others came too.

The Gypsies watched the round black rabbit hole where Chris had gone, and waited. Gypsies were used to waiting.

'Look,' said little Minta.

Through the square yellow window they saw a great green tree dressed up like a Gypsy princess with shining red and gold and a thousand coloured lights.

'Gaujé is mad as magpies,' Pattella said, and then there was a scuffle of feet and Gaujé kids came popping out of the rabbit hole and lined up in front of them.

'Told you,' said Chris breathlessly.

'What's Miss Lee going to say?' said June.

'Going to have kittens, isn't she?' said Dusty.

'What you want to come here for?' said Mary fiercely.

'New boy, isn't he?' said Chris indignantly. 'You don't talk like that to a new boy.'

'They can't all be in Class Six,' said Ron.

'She's got ear-rings,' said Mary, pointing to Pattella's ears.

'She can't come to school in ear-rings, can she?'

Pattella grinned her toothless grin and shook her head so her ear-rings rattled.

'What we going to do?' said Chris.

Liberty's black eyes slid back and forth between the pink Gaujé mouths. He only understood part of what they were saying, but at least they were safe from the gavvers for the moment. Couldn't move 'em off till a day and a dark-time after the 'viction order.

Suddenly a bell rang loud and clanging close, and the Lovells screamed and pressed back against the wall with hands to their ears, and the Gaujé came out like ants from an ant-hill. It was break.

'Aren't they little ducks?' Rosie said going down on her knees, and everybody crowded round the Gypsy children.

'Lovely little things, aren't they?' Linda said looking at Bella. 'Pong a bit though.'

'It's only wood-smoke,' June said.

'Mine's got a red cardigan and a blue skirt,' said Rosie as if Minta was a doll.

'Mine's got a mauve jersey and a black skirt and no shoes,' said Linda. 'What's yours got underneath?'

'Leave 'em,' Liberty hissed furiously. 'Leave 'em be.'

'All right, all right,' said Linda.

'What we going to do?' said Chris. 'Can't just stand here looking at them.'

'First thing is to give 'em a good wash,' said Rosie. 'Bet they never had a proper wash all their lives.'

'Don't you touch 'em,' Liberty shouted, and he jumped forward with his teeth bared and his black eyes flashing. A Gaujo would pat a dog, Ma said. The Gaujo was not clean.

'You keep your dirty hands off us, you,' Liberty shouted.

'Hark who's talking!' Rosie said.

'Better get 'em down to the cloakroom,' said Chris, and the Gypsy children followed him down the black rabbit hole. Liberty zigzagged like a fox was behind him and his black eyes were wide and scared.

Mr Beach sat cross-legged on the table, playing his record again. 'They've come,' shouted Chris.

'Oh Lord,' said Mr Beach, pushing his fair hair out of his eyes and looking at the six Gypsy children. Wait till Julie heard about this.

'Shall I fetch Miss Lee?' said Mary primly.

'I'll go,' said Mr Beach. He walked up the stairs, and Tom stood inside the square he had made for his inn. 'They're not coming in my inn.'

'You shut up,' said Chris, glaring at Tom. 'He's a new boy, isn't he?'

'He's a Gypsy,' said Tom.

'Can't all be in Miss Lee's class,' said June. 'Little ones are too small for the Infants even.'

'How old are you, love?' Rosie asked Minta, bending close, and the four little Gypsy girls pushed back into the swinging coats and covered their faces.

'It's not very nice them touching our things,' Mary whispered, and Tom licked his felt pen and started to write.

'They could be in the play; little angels with white wings,' said June.

'Us don't want no play, us want to write like Gaujé,' Liberty scowled.

'There you are,' said Tom. He had finished writing and now he stood back triumphantly and put the notice he had written on the end of the bench. *No Gypsies Served Here*.

It was June snatched the notice and crumpled it, and her face was pink. 'I don't want Gypsies coming in my inn,' shouted Tom.

'They got to go somewhere,' shouted Chris, clenching his fists.

'Somewhere else,' shouted Tom, and then everyone was shouting.

'Just because Tom's mum doesn't like Gypsies,' Linda shouted.

'Your mum signed the letter, didn't she?' Tom shouted, and it wasn't fair, everyone turning on him. 'And so did yours, Chris Jenkins. Nobody wants Gypsies on the dump. Nobody.'

Miss Lee and Mr Beach and Mr Page came down the stairs, and at once everybody was quiet. The little Gypsy girls were quite hidden by the coats, but Liberty stood there clenching his fists and scowling under his hat fringe. He hated this shut-in place; the Gaujé squabbled like dogs with a bone, and the pale eyes of the Gaujé teachers fell on his body like cold rain.

'Take your hat off then, lad,' said Mr Page.

'Naw,' said Liberty, and he clamped his hat down firmly with one arm and glared out through the white fringe like an animal through grass.

Class Six gasped, but Mr Page said amiably. 'Where do you come from, lad?'

'Forgot,' said Liberty. The Gaujé was all questions and it was best to tell them nothing, Ma said.

'Please, sir,' said Chris. 'Mr Beach says the Gypsies come from India.'

'Naw,' said Liberty, frowning because he'd never heard of India or any place like it. 'Amersham way, us come from.'

'How old are you?' asked Mr Page, and this Liberty really didn't know for sure. He jerked his head towards his sisters hidden in the coats. 'Older'n this lot,' he said.

Miss Lee and Mr Beach and Mr Page went back to the stairs and talked in low voices, and everybody crowded round the Gypsy children.

'You hungry?' Dusty said, and he got out his biscuits from his cold lunch tin. The little Gypsy girls came out of the coats and clutched the biscuits in their red-stained hands.

'Tomorrow I'm going to bring sugar biscuits with nursery rhymes for them,' Linda said.

'So am I,' said Rosie.

'I'm going to finish that African blanket,' June said.

'What's the sense of a blanket if they haven't got a place to stop?' said Chris, and little Minta began to whimper.

Liberty scowled and said, 'Us wanna write us name.'

'All right,' said Chris, and he picked up Tom's crumpled notice from the floor and spread it clean side up. 'Sit down. You'll have to take your hat off.'

'Naw,' said Liberty, but he sat down on the bench and Chris sat beside him with the felt pen and got in under Liberty's hat brim and wrote LIBERTY in big black letters.

'Now you write each letter underneath,' said Chris, and Liberty took the pen tight in his hand and marks came on the page black and straggly as spiders.

'You got to do it lots of times,' said Chris.

8 The first rehearsal

The Lovells were joining the 'Greens' for the moment, Mr Beach said, and Chris jumped up and shouted, 'Welcome to Class Six, Liberty Lovell and Pattella and . . . all the others.'

'I call that barmy when they're too small for the Infants even,' Dusty muttered, and Minta began to cry.

'They ought to get the school nurse to look at their hair,' Mary said, and Pattella pulled Minta on to her knee and began to rock her back and forth.

'The Gypsies ought to be in the Christmas play,' said June. 'They could all be little angels couldn't they?'

'Well they're not coming in my inn,' muttered Tom, 'Angels or no angels.'

Liberty went on writing under his hat, and Mary held up the baby doll. 'I bags I'm Mary.'

'It's not fair,' said Linda. 'She was Mary year before, year before last.'

Mr Beach rubbed his marigold hair and wondered which one was the most likely to cry, and Pattella rocked Minta in her arms and sang softly in her own Romany tongue. It was a wailing little song that Ma sang, and in the cloak-room everything went very quiet. 'You shut your trap, Pattella,' Liberty hissed. He didn't like the Gaujé listening to a Gypsy song.

'Pattella ought to be Mary,' Chris whispered, and his eyes were bright. 'Pattella for Mary,' he shouted.

'Pattella for Mary,' shouted Dusty and Ron, jumping up and down.

'That's a smashing idea,' said Mr Beach. 'A Gypsy Mary.' Julie could get some good photographs for the *Mercury*.

'She's all brown and she's got ear-rings,' Mary said furiously.

'Not having blinkin' Gypsies in our Christmas play,' shouted Tom.

'Anyway she doesn't know *Away in a Manger*,' said Linda.

'She can sing her own Gypsy song,' said June.

'It was a beautiful song,' said Mr Beach. 'Will you sing it for us again?'

Pattella glanced quickly at Liberty and shook her head.

'Can't be Mary then, can she?' said Linda.

'Anyway she's not stopping,' said Mary under her breath, and Tom frowned. There was no sense letting on that Mum was round the Town Hall already, not when everybody was on the Gypsy's side.

'Pattella is Mary,' said Mr Beach.

'Hurrah,' said Chris and Dusty and Ron. Under his hat Liberty frowned and went on writing, and June got Pattella dressed up in the blue robe and Rosie started teaching her *Away in a Manger*. Mr Beach explained what he had found out at the Town Hall. Three months ago the Council had discussed making a winter site but there had been so little 'public interest' they had decided to wait. Now the winter camp site was going to be discussed again at the next Council meeting on Friday. They'd send tickets for the play to all the Council Members. A Gypsy Mary would show there was 'public interest' all right. It was a great idea.

Chris wore a brown robe and he had a long stick and the African blanket, all coloured squares, round his shoulders, and a twist of red and gold material round his head. Miss Lee had come down to see how the rehearsal was going.

'Where's the play? What am I supposed to say?' said Chris. Mr Beach explained that Mary and Joseph and the innkeeper just said what they wanted to say. June was going to write it down and that would be the play. Then he put on the Eastern music, quite soft, and June sat down with her pencil ready.

Chris took a deep breath and said, 'This is my poor wife, Mary. She's ever so tired. She's come a long way and she's ever so tired.'

'Us is tired,' said Pattella, and everybody was looking at her and it was exciting, and she grabbed a cushion and pushed it down the front of her cardigan, and then she grabbed the African blanket from Chris and put it over her head.

'Mary has to be in blue,' Mary whispered.

'You shut up,' said Chris fiercely.

'Get on with it,' said Mr Beach glancing at Miss Lee.

'Us is very tired. Mary is ever so . . . ever so tired,' Pattella said in a loud sing-song voice. She walked up and down the cloakroom with her cushion belly pushed right out. She liked everybody watching and she knew more about babies than any Gauji girl, didn't she?

'Oh dear!' said Miss Lee.

'My poor wife is tired,' Chris said. 'We've come a long way. We've been to pay our taxes.'

'Didn't know they had taxis those days?' muttered Ron.

'Hush,' said June. 'I can't write that.'

'Us tired, ever so tired,' said Pattella limping on Chris's arm. 'Poor Mary is tired.'

'Get on the donkey then,' muttered Dusty.

'Can't,' said Pattella. ' 'Er's too big.'

Ron got down on his knees, and Pattella sat on his back. 'Can't get up now, can I?' Ron groaned.

Dusty pushed and Chris pushed. Then Ron was up, and Pattella was sitting on the floor in the middle of the grey blanket.

'Oh dear,' said Miss Lee, and round the walls the 'Reds' and 'Blues' tittered. 'When I think of all those important people . . .'

'Start again,' shouted Mr Beach. 'And just lead the donkey.'

'We ought to be singing in the inn,' Tom said. 'Like round at The Bull.'

'Look there's an inn,' said Chris, and Pattella leaned on his arm, and her hair smelt of wood-smoke and the donkey trotted behind them.

Chris knocked at the inn. 'Is there anybody there?' he shouted, but before Tom could reply Liberty sprang on to the stage. 'Us done 'er,' he shouted, and he put the piece of paper into Miss Lee's swollen hands.

Miss Lee gazed wonderingly at the wild, black scribble. 'You wrote this?'

'Liberty,' Liberty shouted. 'Us wrote 'er good as any Gaujo.'

9 'That clanging goes right through my head'

'That's very nice,' Miss Lee said and everyone crowded round to look. The little Gypsy girls came out of the coats and blinked their black eyes at Liberty's writing. 'Now you must learn to write "Lovell".'

'There's Lovell's in the High Street,' said Dusty.

'He ought to have an Indian name,' said Ron.

'Gypsies used to find out the most important person in the district,' Mr Beach said, 'and take his name.'

'Never took nothing,' Liberty scowled.

'Let's see this marvellous writing then,' said Tom, and Liberty stepped into the square of benches and held the paper out proudly. Tom peered at the black letters, moving it near and away like a man playing a trombone. 'Can't read it,' he said. 'What's it say then?'

'He's written his name,' June said.

'What's so wonderful about that?' said Tom. 'We've been writing our names since the Infants, haven't we?'

'But Liberty has never been to school, Tom,' said Miss Lee.

'Who's fault's that?' said Tom, getting angry and pink again because everybody had gone on Liberty's side. 'He's a dirty rotten Gypsy thief,' Tom shouted, and he pushed Liberty hard in the chest. 'You get out of my inn, you, I'm not having Gypsies coming in my inn.'

'Cut that out, Tom,' said Mr Beach, grabbing both boys.

'Tom, Tom, whatever is the matter?' Miss Lee said, and suddenly Tom dropped down on the bench and covered his face with his hands.

'He's crying,' Rosie whispered wonderingly, and everybody stared. Nobody had seen Tom cry, not since the Infants anyway.

'It's the police been on to him,' Rosie explained, and tears popped into her eyes. Rosie couldn't bear it when anybody cried.

'Must have been the holly,' said Chris.

'What holly?' said Mr Beach, and Tom looked up with his face all wet and his eyes swollen.

'Stole the holly from the lady's garden, didn't he?' Tom said pointing at Liberty. 'Just took it, didn't he? But it was me copped it, it was me the police fetched round the station, and I said I was at school but they didn't listen to me, only my mum made them listen all right,' said Tom, and he buried his face in his arms with the misery of it, sitting there in the Police Station and everyone thinking him a thief.

Liberty's black eyes gleamed under the white fringe. Fancy the gavvers getting on to a Gaujo boy; nice change that.

'I'm going to get right to the bottom of this holly business,' Miss Lee said, and Mr Beach pushed his hair out of his eyes and said, 'I'm afraid travelling people aren't always . . .'

Miss Lee said, 'Did you take the holly, Liberty?'

'Never took nothing,' Liberty scowled. The Gaujé stared with their pebble-eyes, and he was stuck there like a baby rabbit in a nest of weasels, and he measured the jump to the stairs.

'He did,' Tom shouted.

'Course he did,' shouted Mary, and she swung the baby doll at Liberty's shoulder. 'Got our Tom into trouble, didn't you?'

'Leave him,' shouted June.

'He was hungry, wasn't he?' shouted Chris. 'Who chucked his buns in the gutter?'

'I never did,' Tom shouted furiously.

'Be quiet, both of you,' said Miss Lee sharply. 'Liberty, perhaps you'd better tell us about the holly?'

'Just growing, weren't 'er?' Liberty mumbled.

Everywhere there was sky and grass and bushes and berries for everybody but how you going to tell that to a Gaujo? He looked helplessly at Pattella and she pushed forward.

'Christmas time is Christmas flowers,' Pattella began in a sing-song voice. 'Springtime us picks primroses and sells 'em and then 'ers daffs in the woods, isn't 'er? Primroses ain't for the Gaujé. Primroses is for Gypsy or Gaujo or anybody as wants to pick 'un, and 'ers 'olly in the woods and furze and bluebells and gilty-cups and all.'

'That's all very well in the woods and fields,' Miss Lee said, and then the hammering started. It rang out from the dump, clean and clear as a bell. Pa was back with the old wagon and one of the cars left at the roadside when the gavvers come. Now there was a car to break, Liberty thought, and his heart lifted. That was a man's job with a hammer and a crowbar and a great clang-clang, that was better'n any Gaujo writing.

'Whatever is that noise?' Miss Lee said.

' 'Ers Pa,' Liberty grinned proudly. 'Us gotta go and 'elp 'un.'

'You can't just go in and out of school when you like,' said Miss Lee, but Liberty was already at the door, and the little Gypsy girls scampered after him. Pattella clutched the African blanket under her chin.

'Pattella's in the play, ain't 'er?' she said. 'Pattella's not coming.'

'You come quick,' Liberty said, and he raised a threatening fist.

'Leave her,' Chris shouted. 'Pattella, you stop here.' But Pattella pouted and walked slowly towards the stairs, dropping the African blanket and the cushion and the blue robe as she went.

'Can't be Mary if she goes off in the middle, can she?' said Mary, grabbing the blue robe. Mr Beach crossed the floor with two scissor steps of his long legs and caught hold of Pattella's arm. 'Listen,' he said, and clang-clang went the hammering and Liberty scowled from the top of the stairs. 'Pattella's got to be in the play,' said Mr Beach. 'The play is on Thursday, and people are coming from the Council, and there'll be pictures in the paper and then a Council Meeting next day to discuss the winter site for the Gypsies.'

'Council's Gaujo ain't 'er?' Liberty growled. 'Gaujo don't help Gypsy. "Hairs growin' on a diamond first".'

'That clanging goes right through my head,' Miss Lee murmured.

'Let us stay,' Pattella whispered, and her small brown hands begged Liberty, and it didn't do to turn away good luck, Ma said.

'You stop here, you, and don't talk to no Gaujo,' he said roughly, and then he was gone across the playground and scrambling over the wall.

Clang-clang went Pa's hammer and the old wagon was there and the lorry and the car, left at the roadside when the gavvers towed 'em off. Strips of dark blue metal lay on the ground.

The little girls went in the wagon after Ma. Hopsy, the youngest Lovell, tottered in the mud and turned his head at Liberty's footsteps and fell among the old tins, his black eyes startled, and Liberty rubbed his curly black head. 'Us got the old car then?' Liberty said, and the sweat was running down to the red dicklo round Pa's neck.

'Us got to get 'er broke afore dark-time,' Pa said.

'Liberty's going to help,' said Liberty, but Pa shook his head. 'You go to your Ma.' Pa stopped hammering then, and in the silence Liberty heard crying. Ma was crying.

'Baby, is 'er?' Liberty whispered.

'Gavvers,' Pa said. ''Viction order. Pushed 'er under door.' Gavvers was like bulldogs, Liberty thought, they never let go.

'Us gotta get 'er scrap sold afore dark-time,' Pa said.

'Us got nowhere to go,' said Liberty. 'And nowhere to stop.'

Loud clanging came from the dump and Chris was worried. Mrs White and Mrs Jones wouldn't stand for a noise like that in their back yards.

'My head's splitting,' Miss Lee moaned.

After dinner they did scene two with the shepherds sitting round their fire, which was a torch underneath red crepe paper and some sticks. Mr Beach got Linda to lie down and switch the torch on and off, so it really did look like a flickering fire. The 'Blues' were the sheep bleating, and it really was like sheep on a dark hill, Chris thought, except for the clanging on the dump.

'What about the bright star?' Chris said, and Mr Beach asked Mary to be the bright star. She stood on a chair behind the black blanket and held Ron's bicycle lamp over the top.

'That's a very nice bright star,' Mr Beach said.

Scene three was the stable. Chris leaned on his stick and looked down at Pattella. The baby Jesus was just a bundle of overalls, and Pattella held it because they hadn't got a manger yet. Chris felt sort of proud, just as if it really was his wife and baby, and sad too because they had nowhere to go and the baby was born in a stable.

How could he help the Gypsies? Chris wondered. Pattella had big black eyes and wrists like sticks, and Liberty was his friend and wore a cowboy hat and didn't care for anyone. Then Chris thought of the letter. Mrs White had written a letter. Well Chris could write a letter, couldn't he?

'Listen, Pattella,' Chris whispered, and his eyes were bright with the letter idea, but the bell went and everybody was shouting and scrambling out of their costumes. Pattella grinned her toothless grin and went towards the stairs.

'Come back here, you,' Chris shouted like Liberty shouted. But Chris wasn't her brother, wasn't even a Gypsy, and Pattella ran up the stairs and away across the playground.

'I got this letter idea,' Chris said to Mr Beach. 'What about I write a letter asking for a winter site for the Gypsies and get people to sign?'

'Great idea,' said Mr Beach, ducking his head to look out of the window and only half-listening. Julie was coming, and she wanted to get some pictures of the Gypsies camping on the dump. Make a real front page story of it.

'See you,' said Mr Beach, as Julie's car drew up at the pavement.

Chris stood on the cloakroom stairs. The school was almost empty and the caretaker's broom thumped in the classroom. Somebody had switched out the lights. In the darkness voices whispered.

'Leave your baby Jesus on the peg, stupid,' whispered Tom.

'I'm not letting any Gypsy have him,' Mary whispered.

'Gypsies'll be gone before tomorrow,' Tom said. 'Mum told us, didn't she?' Mary wrapped the doll in her jersey and laid him gently at the top of her peg. 'Don't want him catching cold,' she murmured.

'Come on,' said Tom irritably.

Chris stepped back into the dark passage as they ran up the stairs and went out across the playground. He switched on the cloakroom light. His heart was thumping with alarm. How did Mrs White know the Gypsies would be off the dump tomorrow? He lifted the doll off Mary's peg and stared at its blank pink face.

'I'd like to ring your blinkin' neck,' he muttered.

'Here! What you doing with that doll?' said Mr Davis, shuffling down the stairs.

'Nothing,' said Chris.

10 Chris's letter

It was colder again and the dark grey sky had the yellowish look of snow. Chris ran along the pavement and the thoughts whirled in his head. Gypsies be gone before tomorrow, what did Tom mean?

Above the whirr of the evening traffic came the clang-clang of the Gypsy's car-breaking. At the bus stop the people turned up their coat collars and stared across the dump. 'Wouldn't fancy living next to that lot.'

Julie's car was parked between the boarded-up shops, and Chris pushed past it. The dog snarled and jumped at the end of its chain, and the windows of the caravan glowed red. It was getting dark. A fire crackled on the other side, and Liberty and his father worked by its light. Julie and Mr Beach stood by uncertainly, but the Gypsies took no notice of them.

'It's too dark for pictures,' Julie said, swinging the camera strap. She had a long leather coat with fringes at the bottom and shoulders. 'Have to come back tomorrow morning.'

'But you got a flash-bulb,' said Chris urgently. 'The Gypsies'll be gone tomorrow. Couldn't you just try?'

'Julie's the photographer, isn't she?' said Mr Beach. 'And if she says tomorrow . . .'

'Tomorrow's too late,' Chris said, and then his voice sank to a whisper. 'They're going to move the Gypsies off. Tom White's mum said.'

'What does she know?' said Mr Beach.

Julie looked at the backs of the houses. 'With this row they'll be waking babies for miles round,' she said.

Mr Beach pushed back his marigold hair. 'Perhaps we'd better have a word with them,' he said doubtfully.

Liberty saw them coming all right but he went on working, flinging the strips of metal into the back of the lorry. The light metal wasn't worth much; it was the engine and the heavy frame that was worth the money. They'd work all through the dark-time, till the car was broke or the gavvers came. Only what did the Gaujé want? Liberty watched them sideways under the brim of his hat.

'Good evening,' Mr Beach said.

'Evening,' said Pa pushing hard on the crowbar, his forehead beaded with sweat.

'Your lad here learned to write his name this afternoon,' said Mr Beach. Liberty scowled, and flung another bit of metal into the lorry with a resounding clang. Liberty didn't care for anyone, Chris thought, not teachers or anyone.

'Tomorrow I want to take some photos of your family here on the dump,' said Julie, and Pa Lovell looked up with the crowbar in his hand and said, 'Cost you a bit, that will.'

'You don't understand,' said Julie. 'I work for a newspaper, the *Mercury*. I want to get everybody interested in a winter site for Gypsies.'

Pa Lovell spat on the ground and swung the crowbar. 'Gaujo helping Gypsy? "Hairs growin' on a diamond first",' he said.

'Still you don't want to upset people, do you?' said Mr Beach. 'All this loud clanging at this time of night?'

'Breakin' cars is us living, ain't 'er?' Pa Lovell growled. 'Us got to get 'er broke quick.'

'But it makes people angry and then they'll turn you off quick,' Chris said desperately. Liberty looked at Chris. This Gaujo boy was all right for a Gaujo, he thought, but they got the 'viction order already and what was the use of talk? The Gaujé were all talk.

'Us got to get the car broke quick,' Liberty said. He tossed another metal strip into the back of the lorry, and his black eyes gleamed in the firelight.

Dusty was serving in the corner shop while his dad had a cup of tea. Chris slid down behind the bacon counter out of sight.

'Give us a bit of paper, will you? I got to write this letter. People are going to sign with all this noise going on, stands to reason.'

'I dunno about that,' said Dusty, flicking his spectacles up his nose. Mrs Jones came into the shop.

'Half a pound of cheese, please,' she said.

'Paper?' whispered Chris.

'Certainly, Mrs Jones,' said Dusty, letting a large piece of wrapping paper float to the floor. Need a good sized bit of paper for all the signatures, Chris thought. He licked his pencil and started to write, *We, the undersigned, want the Council to . . .*

'Half a pound of butter, please, Dusty,' said Mrs Jones. 'Oh that dreadful clanging.'

'Yeah,' said Dusty, and Chris gripped his ankle tight under the counter. 'Awful, isn't it?'

'Given me one of my headaches,' said Mrs Jones.

'Leggo,' Dusty said, as Chris gripped tighter.

'I beg your pardon?' said Mrs Jones.

'Asp'rin?' said Dusty, leaping on to the shelf steps. 'Used to be some asp'rin up the top. Very good for headaches.'

'It's disgraceful,' said Mrs Jones.

'Absolutely disgraceful,' Mr Miller said, coming back into the shop.

'We don't seem to have any asp'rin,' said Dusty from the ladder, and Chris stuck out his tongue.

'Never mind,' said Mrs Jones. 'Won't be for long.'

'Hope not,' said Mr Miller, opening the door for Mrs Jones and shutting it behind her.

'What she mean by that?' said Chris.

'Search me,' said Mr Miller. 'Customer's always right in this shop.'

'Aren't Gypsies customers?' said Chris.

'Not in here they're not,' said Mr Miller. 'I'd lose every bit of trade I got if the Gypsies came in here.'

Chris stood up and spread his letter on the bacon counter. 'I've written asking the Council to put a camp site for the Gypsies somewhere else, so they won't stay on the dump,' said Chris. 'You going to be the first to sign, Mr Miller?'

'Not me, lad,' said Mr Miller. 'Signed Mrs White's letter, didn't I? More'n my life's worth to sign yours.'

'I'm a customer, aren't I?' said Chris. 'Last time I come in here for bubble gum.' He banged out of the shop. It was cold outside and quite dark. June was coming down the High Street with Rags.

'You going to sign my letter?' Chris said.

'Can't see, can I?' June said, and she took it into the phone box. Rags whined and sat down. 'Mrs White says they're going to move the Gypsies off right away,' Chris said.

'Still *your* letter's going to cancel out *her* letter, isn't it?' June said. 'Only you'd better ring up and tell them then.'

'Who?' said Chris.

'The Council, silly. Ring 'em up at the Town Hall.'

'Well I could,' said Chris doubtfully. 'You got any money?'

'I was going to get a choc bar,' June said, but she took out her purse. He didn't want them thinking he was just some silly kid, Chris thought, trying out a voice half-muffled behind his hand while June dialled the Town Hall. Somebody lifted the receiver the other end and Chris pushed his money in and said in a deep voice, 'This is Mr Jenkins. I want to speak to the er . . . housing department.'

'I'll put you through,' a girl's voice said, and the seconds ticked on and Rags whined, and then a man said, 'Housing department.'

'This is Mr Jenkins,' Chris growled into the phone. 'It's about the Gypsies on the dump. I got this letter and everybody's signed it and . . .'

The voice at the other end interrupted smoothly, 'The matter has already been taken care of, sir.'

'What do you mean "taken care of"?' Chris's voice shot up an octave with alarm. 'My letter says . . .'

'I don't think you'll be troubled with the Gypsies much longer, sir,' said the voice, and the phone began a frantic bleep.

'Got any more money?' said Chris.

'No,' said June, and then the phone went dead.

'He got the wrong end of the stick,' said Chris desperately. 'He thought I was wanting the Gypsies put off. We'd better get round the Town Hall right away.'

'Quarter to six,' shouted June as they raced down the High Street. The Town Hall clock floated above the roofs like a patterned moon. Rags sat down on the pavement.

'You're a dead loss, you are,' Chris muttered, bundling the old dog under his arm.

It struck six just as they got to the Town Hall. People were streaming out between the great white pillars as Chris and June ran up the flight of steps. Just as they reached the top the great door clanged shut.

'Excuse me,' Chris shouted banging on the door with his fists. 'I gotta see somebody. There's been a mistake . . .' But the door didn't open. They sat down at the top of the steps.

'Fat lot of good that was,' Chris said.

'You might as well put the letter through the door now you're here,' June said.

'It's only got your name and mine,' said Chris.

'We could put Rags Jenkins,' said June.

'Very funny,' said Chris. 'And Little Red Riding Hood, too, I suppose?' And suddenly he had an idea and his eyes brightened. 'Why don't I put Mrs Jones and Mrs White and everybody?'

'You'll get into trouble,' said June.

'I don't care,' said Chris. 'Liberty's my friend, isn't he? And Pattella too.' He spread the letter on the steps and began to write. 'Amy White, 25 The Terrace . . .'

'You'll catch it,' whispered June.

'I don't care,' said Chris, sloping his writing a different way. 'I bet I get more signatures than Mrs White.'

The old car was broken up and the last piece landed in the back of the lorry with a metallic clang.

'Done 'er, ain't us,' said Pa Lovell cheerfully, and Liberty piled more wood on the fire and grinned. Plenty of wood and the old car broke and the stew-pot filled with the holly money and cooking on the fire. It was good luck, Liberty thought, the Lovell's luck was changed.

Ma came out in her old black shawl and her hands red-stained from the Christmas flowers, and Pattella carried Hopsy, half-asleep with his black head tucked against her shoulder. They threw more wood on the fire, so it was like a fiery hill, and the sparks went up into the darkness.

Chris stood between the boarded-up shops, he had wanted to tell Liberty about the letter, good as a Gypsy trick, wasn't it? Now he stood in the cold darkness but he didn't go close. The Gypsies had nowhere to stop but they were having a party. They crouched round the fire that was big enough to put smuts like black pennies on everybody's washing, and Ma stirred the great stew-pot. Chris stood in the darkness and watched them. There were lights in the bedroom windows around. Mrs White and Mrs Jones and Mrs Miller were watching too; everybody round the dump was watching.

The Gypsies began to sing. Each child had an empty tin and rapped the rhythm on the bottom with her knuckles. It sounded like drums, and the drumming and the singing called to Pattella and she got up to dance. She whirled and twisted in the firelight, and Pa clapped and Ma screeched with joy because the Gaujé watched like weasels and wasn't one of 'em with a girl could dance like her Pattella danced, with the rhythm of the wagon in her blood.

Liberty frowned. The eviction order was in his hand and he pressed it against his tin and wrote 'Liberty'.

'Our Liberty writes like a Gaujo,' Ma cried, and her screeching laugh was like the startled jaybird. Liberty crumpled the Gaujo paper and threw it on the fire where it curled and died in the red flames. Took more than a Gaujo eviction order to get a Gypsy down.

Liberty stood up to sing, shouting his song into the darkness so the Gaujé houses shook.

Can you mend a kettle?
Can you mend a pot?
Can you cook a channy
When the fire is hot?

11 Early one morning

Liberty sat up in the darkness. He was sleeping in the old wagon under the big bed at the end. Above him Pattella and Bella breathed softly, but from the darkness outside came shouts and then the revving of an engine and Ma's voice screamed high and shrill. The gavvers had come.

Liberty slept fully clothed, and now he scrambled out and groped for his hat. It was dark-time but the gavvers had come with their torches and their tractor.

'Want yer eyes blacked do yer? Want yer nose broke do yer?' Ma screeched as she stood on the steps of the blue wagon with Hopsy asleep in her arms and Minta clinging to her skirts. The dog jumped and snarled at the end of its chain.

'Us Gypsies got nowhere to go,' Ma wailed into the cold darkness.

Liberty jumped down from the wagon, shivering in the dark-time wind, and untied the dog. Gavvers were everywhere, and Pa was talking to them, wheedling and then shouting. Liberty cuffed the dog quiet and crouched beside the den and waited. It was always like this when the gavvers put them off.

There was a clattering from the street and the tractor came across the pavement. There was a Gaujo driving it with a wool cap over his ears. Ma shrieked and the little girls wailed, and Liberty's lips curled back from his teeth and he spat on the muddy ground.

'Take the small un first, Harry,' somebody shouted, and Liberty dived into the old wagon and shook Pattella and Bella awake, and they tumbled out as the Gaujo hooked the old wagon to the tractor and dragged it across the dump and into the street. Broke 'er last time, didn't 'er? Liberty thought. Gaujé slept safe as maggots in their warm beds.

The tractor came bouncing back over the tins and boxes and hitched up the blue wagon. Pa crossed to the lorry and the little girls ran after him. Ma stood on the wagon steps and cursed the police, wild and screeching in her own tongue.

'Go on with your husband, missus,' the policeman said kindly enough, but there were tears in Ma's eyes and Liberty leapt up snarling. 'Leave 'er, you.' Liberty took Hopsy, and Ma leaned on his shoulder. The old lorry whirred and coughed in the cold dark and Ma groaned and heaved herself up to the cabin and Liberty scrambled up with Hopsy. Pa revved loud and the old green lorry hurtled across the dump, rattling like bones in a tin can. On the pavement the gavvers jumped back.

It was the noise of the tractor woke Chris and he got out on to the cold lino. He saw the wagon towed off. Hadn't they had his letter then? Chris dressed quickly. Everybody else had let the Gypsies down, so now it was up to him.

June turned over as Chris opened the door and her square of red knitting slid on to the floor but she didn't wake. There was a faint smell of sausages on the dark stairs. Chris put on the kitchen light and Rags yawned in his basket.

'You go back to sleep,' Chris whispered, taking a packet of cornflakes. 'It's the middle of the night.'

The cold wind was like a knife against his cheek and Chris drew in his breath sharply. The Town Hall clock showed half-past four as he ran down the High Street. He knew somewhere the Gypsies could stop, didn't he?

A car came round the corner and Chris dodged into the dark doorway of the Co-op and stayed still as the car went past. It was a police car.

Chris ran round the corner and into Kings' Street, as the lorry came rattling towards the traffic lights with the blue wagon hooked behind and Pa Lovell at the wheel.

'Hey,' Chris shouted, and he ran across the road waving his arms. 'Hey.'

The lorry didn't stop, but Chris ran beside it. He thumped on the door with his fists. 'Hey, Liberty.'

The Lovells were packed like sardines in the small front cabin and the side window was misted white from their breath. Liberty rubbed a circle clean and looked down at Chris, but still the lorry didn't stop.

But Chris was determined once he had an idea and now he grabbed the door handle and wrenched it open; the lorry stopped abruptly.

'What you want, you?' Liberty said roughly, and the Lovells stared down at Chris with eyes like black stones.

'Where are you going?' Chris shouted.

'Us got nowhere to go.'

'I know a place,' said Chris eagerly. 'I'll show you.' He pushed up into the cabin. There was a strong smell of woodsmoke and sweat and nobody moved up for him; but Chris got the door shut somehow.

'Go right at the lights.'

The lorry moved slowly on, and Ma Lovell muttered and

heaved Hopsy to a different part of her lap. The dog sniffed at Chris's ankles and growled softly. Bella nodded at the packet of cornflakes.

'What's 'er got, Gaujo boy?' she whispered, and Chris opened the packet. Ma closed her eyes. Liberty stared out of the window, but the little girls giggled and their brown hands flicked in and out of the packet till the cornflakes were gone.

Pa Lovell drove the lorry down the sloping High Street; the houses were in darkness.

'Left and left again and then right,' said Chris, and his heart thumped with excitement because it was a great idea.

It was still dark when Chris got back to the High Street. The old wagon stood at the side of the road.

'Get us obstruction, next thing,' Pa Lovell muttered, and Chris jumped down and hitched the old wagon to the green lorry, quick as any Gypsy. 'Okay,' he called.

'Won't tell on us will yer?' Pa said out of the lorry window. 'Don't tell nobody where us gone?'

'Course not,' said Chris. 'Cross my heart.' He waved his arm as Pa Lovell rumbled away down the High Street.

The Jenkins's kitchen was warm with frying smells.

'Where you been then?' Mum said as Chris came in. 'Cold morning like this.'

June looked up from her egg and bacon. Her red square of knitting was beside her plate.

'Went for a nice walk, didn't I?' said Chris cheerily.

'Don't be daft,' said Mum. It was pitch black outside the scullery window. 'You been off with the Gypsies, haven't you?'

'They've been towed off the dump,' said Chris defiantly. 'Somebody's got to help them.'

'Where they gone?' said June. 'I'm doing the blanket for them, aren't I?'

'I don't like you going with dirty people like that,' Mum said.

'How they going to get clean without water?' Chris shouted. 'Like to see you keeping clean on a muddy old place like the dump.'

'You'll get a back-hander, my lad, talking to your mum like that,' said Dad.

It was the last day of rehearsal and nearly everybody had brought things for the Gypsy children. Dusty came out of the corner shop as Linda and Rosie went past. Nobody knew that the Gypsies had gone.

'What you got?' Linda said.

'Biscuits,' said Rosie. 'And an old coat of Dad's.'

'I got a bit of cheese from the shop,' said Dusty. Chris and June came down the High Street.

'I got soap,' said Linda. 'I got a nice bit of pink soap.'

'Giving people soap's rude,' said June, and she went off to fetch Dickie.

Chris said nothing, and they went on down Kings' Street and stopped at the dump.

'Where they gone then?' whispered Dusty, and everybody stared at the empty space. There was white frost on the mud and dark wheel marks.

'I dunno,' mumbled Chris because he'd promised Pa Lovell not to tell.

Mr Beach had his orange trousers and yellow shirt and matching yellow tie on again. He came down to the cloakroom for rehearsal and Class Six crowded round.

'The Gypsies have gone off the dump.'

'Gone?' said Mr Beach, looking round for Chris. 'They can't have gone?'

'They've gone all right,' said Chris, going rather pink. 'Went in the night, didn't they?'

'Gone where?' said Mr Beach, and he frowned. Julie would be furious if she couldn't get the photographs.

'I dunno,' mumbled Chris, and Mr Beach looked at him.

'We all brought things,' said Rosie tearfully. 'Biscuits, I brought.'

'Who's going to be Mary?' said Linda, and Mary held her baby doll in her arms and didn't say anything.

'Where have they gone, Chris?' said Mr Beach quietly.

'I dunno,' said Chris and his face was fiery red because he did know but he'd promised not to tell. The Gypsies didn't like the Gaujé knowing where they'd gone and Chris had promised.

'I think you do,' said Mr Beach, and now everyone was looking at Chris.

'Course he does,' said Ron.

'All right, I do,' shouted Chris desperately. 'And I'm not telling.'

'But we all brought things for the Gypsies, didn't we?' said Rosie, holding up her packet of biscuits.

'Can't help that,' shouted Chris.

'How can we help them if we don't know where they've gone?' said Mr Beach.

'Fat lot of help you've been,' muttered Chris, and everybody drew in their breath with a sharp hiss.

'Isn't he rude?' said Mary.

'Don't let anybody talk to him any more,' said Ron.

'Let's send him to Coventry,' said Tom.

It was dark in the cloakroom with the curtains drawn for

scene two: the shepherds and their sheep on the hillside. Chris sat on the stairs and bit his thumb. He wouldn't tell, not if they didn't talk to him for a week, not if they boiled him in oil. Had they got his letter then at the Town Hall? What they going to think when they saw all those names? Liberty didn't care for anyone. Gypsies were like that. Chris wished he was a Gypsy.

'All out,' said Mr Beach, as the bell went for break, and June picked up her square of knitting. Everybody went up the stairs past Chris, just as if he wasn't there. Nobody spoke to him, not even Dusty, but Mary said, 'We're not speaking to you.'

Chris walked slowly up the stairs and across the playground. He didn't care. He heaved himself on to the wall and jumped down on to the dump. There was a cold wind and the ground was hard under his feet. He'd found a place for the Gypsies to stop, hadn't he? He was the only person knew where they were. Chris fitted his foot into the deep ruts of the wheels. Suppose he was to go off and join them? Didn't fancy it this weather but when it got a bit warmer? Must be lovely picking beans and strawberries and plums the summer long, and singing round the fire at night.

'Hallo,' said Julie, and Chris jumped back startled. He hadn't heard her coming, and now she was standing quite close in her leather coat that was all fringes. She smiled, and she had light blue eyes with dark edges round the blue.

'Hallo,' said Chris sullenly, and Julie swung the camera from her shoulder and clicked at the black fire patch and the house backs and the deep ruts.

'What's that for?' said Chris.

'Just background stuff,' said Julie, and her blue eyes looked at Chris thoughtfully. 'Where have they gone then?'

'I'm not telling,' said Chris. 'I promised, didn't I?'

'Well a promise is a promise,' said Julie and she sighed. 'But the *Mercury* comes out Friday and I've got to get the pictures in today.'

'Can't help that,' shouted Chris.

'You know where the Council want to make the Gypsy camp site?' said Julie, and her eyes were like cat's eyes watching him, only they weren't green, and she had a lovely smell like flowers . . .

'Course I don't,' said Chris.

'On the old airfield,' Julie said.

'That's a lie,' spluttered Chris. 'You don't catch me with that one.'

Julie smiled and turned back towards her car, and Chris ran after her. 'Where you going?' he shouted.

'To the old airfield,' she said.

Chris watched the car turn right at the traffic lights, and he blinked rapidly. He hadn't told her, had he? It was his idea and he hadn't told anybody, but what was Liberty going to think? And Pattella?

12 On the airfield

The concrete runway was hard-standing for the wagons, but there was a cruel wind blowing across the airfield. Devil's breath, Ma said, and Pa made a square in front of the huts with the two wagons either end and the old green lorry to keep out the devil's breath.

Pa and Liberty crouched over the fire with mugs of hot sweet tea and the smoke stinging their eyes.

'Got to get off to sell the scrap now,' Pa said, and the roof-felt on the hut heaved and scraped in the wind.

'And fetch the cars?' Liberty said, thinking of the two old cars stuck at the roadside still. School and writing and all Gaujé things had gone out of his head like a slate wiped clean.

'Yeah,' said Pa, and there was a car coming down the lane. Pa stood up. Gaujé didn't leave you alone for a moment, he thought, as the car nosed in through the gap in the hedge. Julie got out with the camera in her hand.

'What you want, you?' Pa said, and Liberty scowled. Julie waved cheerily. As a reporter she was used to people who didn't want to talk to her. It was part of the job. She looked round at the bleak airfield and the broken huts and the wagons parked in a square with the fire in the middle, and her camera clicked.

'Cost you that will,' Pa Lovell growled.

'We want the Council to turn this place into a proper

camping site, don't we?' Julie said, but Gaujé promises were like cushions without feathers, Pa thought.

'Us don't like it 'ere,' Pa Lovell said, and he spat on the hard white concrete.

'Why not?' said Julie. 'You can do what you like out here . . . break cars . . . anything.'

'Er's bad luck, this place,' said Pa.

'Er's weasels,' said Liberty. 'Weasel stood up on 'is back legs and whickered.'

'Weasels don't hurt you,' Julie said, and Liberty scowled. There was no sense arguing with a Gauji, but every Gypsy knew a weasel was bad luck and a whickering weasel was worst luck of all.

' 'Ere, what you doing?' Pa said, as Julie clicked her camera at the closed red curtains and the smoke belching

from the tin chimney and then knocked at the wagon door and stepped inside.

'Nice and warm,' Julie said, glancing at the old Queenie stove. The wagon was full of smoke. Ma Lovell sniffed and muttered and went on working. Hopsy stared at Julie with his thumb in his mouth. The table was littered with wood shavings and half-made Christmas flowers.

'This is beautiful,' said Julie, picking up one finished flower.

'Cost you five pence,' Ma said quickly, and Liberty slipped inside the wagon. Wherever you went, whatever you did, there was the Gaujé asking questions. 'What 'er want?' he scowled.

'I want to take some pictures for my paper. You'd like to have your picture in the paper, wouldn't you?' Julie smiled, and Bella smiled back, but Liberty growled, 'Us don't want no pictures.'

'But you want a proper camp site, don't you?' said Julie.

'Gaujé is all talk,' said Ma, drawing Hopsy on to her knee. 'And us don't like this place. Where us going to sell us Christmas flowers?'

'Sit still,' said Julie, pointing the camera, and the flash-bulb was like lightning, and the little girls squealed with fright, and Ma said roughly, 'You get out of here, you.'

'I want Pattella to come with me,' Julie said.

' "Hairs growin' on a diamond first",' scowled Liberty, as Pa stepped into the wagon. But a place to stop was a place to stop, and the Gaujé were mad as magpies, and it didn't do to cross your luck.

'Liberty and Pattella, you do like the lady say,' said Pa.

Pattella skipped into the front seat. Liberty jammed his hat down on his head. He'd never been in a Gaujo car had he, never been driven by a Gauji woman? He gripped the seat as the engine started, and Ma opened the door and thrust the basket of Christmas flowers inside.

'Sell 'em in the market,' she shouted, but selling was women's work.

' "Hairs growin' on a diamond first",' Liberty muttered.

In the cloakroom of Wood Lane School it was dress rehearsal for the Christmas play. Everybody was helping because they'd only got till tomorrow. In one corner Mr Beach in his yellow shirt was going over scene two with the shepherds. In the inn Tom was trying to teach his guests to sing *Lavender blue dilly dilly*, like Miss Lee said, only the guests said it was a soppy song.

Miss Lee was sticking gold paper crowns for the three kings, and June was putting fruit gum jewels on them.

Dusty and Ron were practising the donkey and the 'Blues' were practising *Hark the Herald Angels Sing*.

Chris sat by himself. He was miserable; nobody would talk to him and, anyway, Julie knew the Gypsies were on the airfield and Liberty would think Chris had told and he hadn't and it wasn't fair.

Feet came hurrying down the stone stairs. It was Liberty in his cowboy hat and Pattella with a great basket of Christmas flowers on her arm, and Julie. There was silence and then everybody was shouting with excitement.

'Pattella for Mary.'

'Where you Gypsies got to?' Ron shouted.

'We got presents,' Rosie shouted, and everybody brought out biscuits and cakes. Rosie gave Liberty her Dad's old coat, but Linda kept the pink scented soap in her pocket. Pattella grinned with her mouth full of biscuit and Liberty collected everything into the basket under the Christmas flowers. Gaujé were as mad as magpies he thought.

'Get into your Mary costume, Pattella,' Mr Beach said, and Chris fetched the blue curtain.

'I didn't tell where you were, honest, I didn't,' he whispered, but Pattella neither cared nor understood the Gaujo boy. She pushed the cushion inside her cardigan. 'You don't need that for scene three, silly,' June said.

Julie turned to Miss Lee. 'I wonder if I can help? I have helped with plays before.'

'We need all the help we can get with this one,' said Miss Lee crisply, as she stuck the last jewel on the last crown. Chris edged his way across to Liberty.

'I didn't tell, honest, I didn't,' he whispered urgently.

Liberty sniffed and then he said, 'Us going to write "Lovell".' Chris grinned with relief and got his rough book and wrote 'Lovell' large and clear.

'We're going on with scene three,' Mr Beach said, and Pattella sat in the centre of the stage with the blue curtain and the African blanket over her head, and Chris stood behind her. They had a wooden box for the manger now and real straw, that Linda was going to take home for her hamster, but they only had a bundle of overalls for the baby. Suddenly Mary said, 'Pattella can have my baby Jesus.' Everybody clapped and Mary passed the baby doll to Chris.

'Thanks,' he whispered, and he put it in the manger. Mary got up on her chair and shone the bright star right on to baby Jesus.

'I done my writing,' Liberty shouted, and he pushed across the cloakroom to Miss Lee with the basket of Christmas flowers on his arm. He held out Chris's rough book.

'"Lovell",' said Miss Lee smiling encouragement, and Liberty wished he'd got a butterfly. Soon cure her chilblains with a butterfly.

'That's very good, Liberty. Can you write "Liberty Lovell" now?' Miss Lee said, and Julie was taking the red Christmas flowers out of the basket and putting them round the baby Jesus in the manger. 'It's a Gypsy Christmas play isn't it?' she said.

'Looks pretty,' said June.

'Lovely,' said Rosie.

'Cost you,' Liberty said.

'How much?' said Miss Lee. 'We have a little money for the Christmas play.'

'One pound to you, lady,' Liberty said in a wheedling tone. 'You gotta lucky face, lady.'

13 A lively Christmas play

'You coming to the Christmas play?' asked June. The warm kitchen smelt of sardines on toast. June packed her mouth as full as she could and then picked up her knitting needles and cast on a new blue square.

'Don't know about your dad?' said Mum.

'Can't get off work three o'clock, can I?' said Dad.

'I'll ask Nan,' said Mum. 'Pity to waste the ticket.'

'We got this Gypsy girl for Mary,' said Chris. There was white frost on the back-yard wall and white frost on the old airfield, Chris thought.

'Bit funny isn't it?' said Mum. 'A Gypsy for Mary?'

'What's funny?' said Chris. 'Mary and Joseph had black hair and they didn't have anywhere to stop.'

'Poor old dog, left by himself all afternoon,' said Dad, and Rags thumped his tail.

Liberty beat his arms across his chest. The frost was like white fur on the black twigs of the hedge, but the wind had hushed its devil's breath and it was a place to stop. Liberty picked up his axe. Got to cut enough wood for the old Queenie stove all day, hadn't he? Above the sound of his chopping came the hoot of an owl. An owl in the daytime was death, Ma said, and she mustn't hear it or they'd have to go. Liberty swung his axe higher and the chips flew, and he began to sing loud as he could in the cold morning.

Can you mend a kettle?
Can you mend a pot?

Liberty's voice rang through the trees and the owl was quiet then, folding its great wings and closing its eyes as the daylight grew brighter.

'Where's your Pa?' said Ma Lovell, sitting up in the great bed across the end of the wagon and straightening her dress. Her grey-black plaits hung loose on her shoulders, and Hopsy lay asleep at her side.

'Gone to sell the scrap and get one of they old cars,' Liberty said, pushing sticks into the stove that burned all night. Ma nodded, and the fire roared in the chimney, and the little girls got out from under Ma's bed and stretched and yawned. When the kettle boiled they drank the strong sweet tea, and Ma spread the white sliced loaf with red jam.

It was almost three o'clock. The 'Reds' were showing people to their places. The hall was full of people all whispering and chattering, except for the front row which was being kept for Mr Page and the people from the Council. Chris twisted the striped stuff round his head. Could they tell if the signatures in his letter were real? Suppose one of the Council was to stand up and ask him about it when he was being Joseph?

'There's our mum, second row back,' said Rosie, peeping through the stage curtains.

'There's our nan,' said Chris.

'Where?' said June, and she knelt down and looked underneath, and there was Mum and Nan in her new green coat. June was prompter; she sat on the edge of the stage and reminded people who forgot their words. Liberty sat beside her, writing his name and scowling because Mr Beach wouldn't let him sit under the Christmas tree.

Everything was ready. Behind the curtain Pattella and Chris waited with the donkey for scene one. Only the donkey kept fidgeting, and Chris's throat felt rather dry. Mr Beach had on his moss-green shirt and there were beads of sweat on his forehead. Miss Lee sat at the piano and rubbed her swollen hands together.

'There's our mum,' whispered Mary, holding the bright star in one hand and peeping through the curtains. Mrs White sat down in the front row, and the 'Reds' pushed each other and said, 'Go and tell her she can't.'

'Look at our mum,' whispered Tom going pink.

Ma Lovell stood in the doorway. She had Hopsy under one arm and a big basket of Christmas flowers on the other. She didn't like this shut-in Gaujo place. Still it was no different from the market really with its glass roof. She swung the basket and walked towards the front row.

'Buy my Christmas flowers? Five pence each. Twenty-five for a bunch of six.' The hall was quiet; everybody stared, and Hopsy put his thumb in his mouth and stared back.

'Oh dear,' said Miss Lee. 'Liberty, I really don't think . . .'

Liberty pulled his hat down and scowled. Ma Lovell sat down in the front row and put a bunch of Christmas flowers on Mrs White's navy-blue lap.

'Only twenty-five pence, lady? You got a lucky face, lady,' she said, and then the Chairman of the Council came in, with a big gold medal on a chain. There were several other men in dark suits, and ladies with flowery hats and smiles. They all sat down in the front row with Mr Page.

'Lights,' shouted Mr Beach. 'Curtains.'

Suddenly it was dark and absolutely quiet, and then Miss Lee played a chord and the 'Reds' started singing *The Holly and the Ivy*, and the curtains slid open and Mr Page said, 'It's rather an experiment.'

Chris's mouth was dry as sand. Had they read his letter? He stared at the faces round as moons, and he couldn't speak.

'Us is ever so tired,' Pattella shouted. She liked all the Gaujé watching her, and she leaned on Chris's arm and limped forward and pulled at the donkey. At first the donkey just stood still, twitching.

It was the hiccups, Dusty said after.

Then the donkey lurched forward. 'Us is ever so tired. Mary is tired,' Pattella shouted, and she gave Chris a hard pinch and he began to speak. 'My poor wife, Mary, is tired, ever so tired,' he said. At first his voice sounded like a key turned in a rusty lock but then it sounded better.

The play went well until Chris said 'There is an inn. Perhaps we can stay there. I'll go and knock.' The knock was the signal for the singing to start in the inn. Some of the guests sang *Lavender blue dilly dilly*, and some sang *The Holly and the Ivy*, and some sang *Roll out the Barrel* because that's what people sang at The Bull.

'Stop that,' Tom whispered, and he pushed his guests. 'Stop that.' Tom went very pink because his mum was just there in the front row. He forgot what he was meant to say, so he didn't say anything.

'I'll go and knock,' Chris said, rather more loudly. He knocked on the bench with his fist and Tom went white, but he still couldn't think what he was *meant* to say and so he said, 'Who's that knocking?'

'You don't say that,' whispered June.

'It's us,' said Chris. 'It's Joseph and Mary. We're poor

people and my wife is ever so tired and we've got nowhere to stop.'

Tom just stood there because he still couldn't remember what to say, and June said in a loud whisper, 'There's no room here. The inn is full.'

'There's no room here. The inn is full,' said Tom.

'May we sleep in your stable?' Chris said.

'Let them sleep with the animals,' said one of the guests, and the others started singing different songs again, and Tom said, 'Stop that.'

'May we sleep in your stable?' said Chris.

'No,' said Tom. 'Go away.'

Chris couldn't go away because Mary and Joseph *had* to sleep in the stable. So he knocked again and said, 'May we sleep in your stable?'

'No . . .' stammered Tom.

'May we sleep in your stable?' said Chris for the third time, and his voice was rather high and squeaky.

'No,' stammered Tom. 'No.'

'You got to let them,' June whispered.

'Show them the stable, Tom,' Mr Beach said quite loudly, and all round the hall there was whispering.

'May we sleep in your stable?' Chris shouted, and Pattella threw herself on the ground with a loud wailing moan. Everybody in the audience was quiet at once and something clicked in Tom's head.

'All right, I'll get my lantern and show you the way,' he said.

All round the hall there was a great sigh of relief. Tom took Mary and Joseph to the stable and the curtains closed for the end of scene one.

'Buy my Christmas flowers, lady?' said Ma Lovell loudly.

'Certainly not,' said Mrs White with her lips very tight.

'Hold 'un then,' said Ma Lovell, and she put Hopsy on to Mrs White's lap and walked along the front row with her basket. 'Buy us Christmas flowers? Five pence each or a bunch for twenty-five,' she shouted.

'Well, I really don't think we . . .' Mr Page began, but one of the ladies said, 'They really are beautiful. Most unusual.' She took twenty-five pence from her handbag.

'You've got a lucky face, lady,' Ma Lovell said.

Then it was time for scene two, and Miss Lee played *While Shepherds Watched their Flocks* and the curtains opened. The three shepherds sat round their flashing red fire that was really Linda and the torch. Ma Lovell waited till the curtains closed again and then she shouted, 'Christmas flowers. Lovely bunch for twenty-five pence.' She sold several bunches and got back to her place just in time for scene three.

'Where's my Hopsy?' she said.

'Hush,' whispered Mrs White. 'He wouldn't stop with me.'

'What 'er done with Hopsy? Hopsy, Hopsy where you gone, you little varmint?' Ma Lovell said loudly. Miss Lee was playing *Hark the Herald Angels Sing* and the curtains opened.

Pattella sat by the manger looking at the baby Jesus lying in his bed of scarlet Christmas flowers, and Chris stood beside her. The shepherds came in and knelt down, and the hall was very quiet.

'Hopsy, Hopsy, where 'un got to?' said Ma Lovell.

'Hush,' said Mrs White.

Then the kings came in with their precious gifts, and then Hopsy came with them.

'Help,' whispered June.

'Leave 'un,' said Liberty, as Dusty tried to get Hopsy

under the donkey's blanket, but Hopsy put his thumb in his mouth and scrambled on to Pattella's lap.

''Er's Hopsy,' said Ma Lovell. 'Hopsy, come 'ere, you little devil.' But Hopsy just sat on Pattella's knee and stared into the darkness of the hall. Suddenly Chris had an idea.

'Look an angel has come to see baby Jesus,' he said.

'Lovely little angel, ain't 'ee?' said Pattella, rocking Hopsy in her arms though he didn't look much like an angel with a fruit gum dribbling down his chin.

Miss Lee began *Away in a Manger* very softly because Pattella was supposed to sing the first verse, but Pattella rocked Hopsy in her arms and began to sing the Gypsy lullaby instead. They'd asked her to sing it and now Ma was there and Hopsy, and Pattella sang the Romany song. She fixed her black eyes on the front row of the hall and sang in a small reedy voice. Miss Lee stopped playing, and Pattella started another verse. This time Ma Lovell sang too and Liberty looked up from his writing and pushed back his hat and sang as loud as he could. The Romany words echoed round the hall, and after that there was deep silence.

Then everybody clapped, and Pattella picked the Christmas flowers out of the manger and gave them to the Chairman of the Council with a nice curtsey. The Chairman of the Council patted her head and Chris jumped down.

'Mary's a Gypsy and the Gypsies got nowhere to stop,' he said breathlessly, but everyone from the front row was going towards the door. The Christmas play was over.

'Went off very well?' Mr Beach said, and Julie nodded and dashed out to get her pictures to the *Mercury*. Behind the stage everybody was taking their costumes off, and Hopsy was picking the fruit gums off the kings' crowns, and Miss Lee had a headache.

'What you got?' Chris said.

'Nothing,' Liberty scowled. 'Ain't got nothing.'

His hand in his pocket felt the hard lines of the square blue flash-bulbs Julie had dropped. Look fine they would on the table with the crystal door knob.

A tortoiseshell butterfly fluttered feeble and shabby against the stage curtains, and suddenly Liberty's arms were waving wildly. He cupped the butterfly between his palms and ran towards Miss Lee.

'Missus,' he shouted. 'Give us your hands, quick. A butterfly is 'er best cure for chilblains.'

14 Christmas party

'Fancy putting Gypsies in the paper,' said Mary, as Mr Beach spread out the two new *Mercurys*. There was a picture of the Gypsies round their fire on the old airfield with the wagon behind them and NO PLACE TO STOP in big black letters. Underneath there was a picture of the dump with all the tins.

'*WOULD YOU like to live here?*' Linda read out. 'No, I wouldn't.'

'Fancy having the old dump in the paper,' said Ron.

'That's our back-yard wall,' said Chris pointing. 'Fancy having our back-yard wall in the paper.'

'Never been anybody I knew in the paper before,' said June gazing wonderingly at Pattella and Liberty and the rest of the Lovells.

'Our Ruby was in the paper, day she got married,' Linda said.

'What about pictures of the play?' said Miss Lee, and Mr Beach said, 'Julie's done us proud.'

In the middle page there was a picture of everybody on the stage at the end, with Hopsy on Pattella's lap and the baby Jesus in his manger full of Christmas flowers.

'That's my feet,' said Ron pointing under the grey blanket.

'Let's put them on the wall,' Chris said, and he took down the African village, dusty and yellow now, and pinned the Gypsies' pictures up instead.

'Do you think they'll be allowed to stay on the airfield?' Chris asked.

Mr Beach flicked back his marigold hair. 'We'll have to wait and see. The Council meeting is at five o'clock, and Julie's going to ring us as soon as she knows.'

'Settle down to work, now,' Miss Lee said.

'Party this afternoon,' Tom whispered, and he looked at Chris. He wished they were friends again.

'Will the Gypsies be coming?' Chris said.

'Course not,' said Tom, and Chris sighed. What did he care about any silly old party if Liberty and Pattella didn't come. Chris stared at the pictures on the wall and Liberty stared back. Would the Gypsies be allowed to stay on the airfield? It was only for the winter, wasn't it? Chris sighed because in the spring he'd still be coming to school each day, and Liberty and Pattella would be out in the fields and moving on and never stopping because Gypsies followed the sun round the earth. That's what Liberty said.

After dinner everybody went home to get the sandwiches and cakes from their mothers. Mrs White brought *her* jellies round on a big tray, pink and green with blobs of cream on top.

'Where we going to sit?' Tom shouted. 'We want the jellies our end.'

'I'm going to sit at the other end,' said Dusty. 'By my mum's sponge cake.'

In the wagon Ma was plaiting Bella's hair, and the other little girls sat in a row with their faces wiped and their hair plaited so tight they couldn't blink their eyes. Minta and Bella had the jerseys that the Gaujé children had brought and Bella had a red flower in her hair and Pattella had the African blanket wrapped round her waist over her ragged skirt. She looked at herself in the mirror behind the crystal door knob. A Gypsy party was a big fire in the dark-time and chickens in the stew-pot and sparks going up into the night and singing and dancing. But what was a Gaujo party?

Liberty fingered the square blue flash-bulbs. Make good buttons for his coat, real nice buttons for a party. only there wasn't any hole in them. He combed his fingers through his hair and looked at his hat.

'Going to sew this for us?' he said to Pattella. The white fringe was loose.

' 'Er's all hitched up,' Pa said, and the Lovells piled into the lorry cabin and Pa started the engine up, and they left the airfield where the devil breathed and weasels whickered, and the lorry moved towards the lane with the wagon trundling behind.

The Gypsy children stared out at the shop windows of the High Street that were all scarlet bells now and white cotton-wool snow. Pa stopped outside Wood Lane School.

Liberty stood in the doorway of the hall. The lights were so bright all over the Christmas tree he had to blink. Everybody was sitting on the floor waiting for Father Christmas and *Jingle Bells* was playing on the record player.

'It's the Lovells,' said Miss Lee.

'Over here,' Chris shouted, and he and June cleared a space, and the Lovells came over and sat down.

'Us come for presents,' Liberty said, and the little girls stared round them. They'd never seen so many Gaujé. Everybody was in the hall, the infants and juniors and teachers, Miss Lee and Mr Beach and Miss Dobson and Mrs

Field. The presents were piled all round the tree, and suddenly Chris thought of something and he crawled over to Miss Lee. 'What about presents for the Lovells?' he whispered.

'Oh my goodness,' said Miss Lee. 'There's extra presents in the staffroom.'

Jingle Bells was playing for the second time as Chris crept up the stairs to the staffroom. There were extra presents on the table because sometimes extra brothers and sisters came to the party. They were already wrapped in red paper and Chris felt them carefully. Two ball point pens, red and blue, would be nice for Liberty, and the nurse's uniform with the red cross on the hat for Pattella, and the little doll in the bed for Minta. A car drew up and Chris looked out of the window. Father Christmas was getting out. Chris scribbled the names in black felt pen and ran down and put them on top of the other presents, just as Father Christmas came into the hall.

He had a scarlet robe and a white beard and big black boots, and he said, 'Ho, ho, ho. Are there any good children here?'

The Infants squealed and went bright pink, and Dickie was bouncing up and down like a jumping bean. Class Six smiled but nobody squealed, and Linda whispered, 'Funny thing that, Father Christmas got a watch like Mr Page's.'

'Hush,' said Miss Lee. 'You don't want to spoil it for the little ones.'

'Ho, ho, ho,' said Father Christmas a few more times, and then he went over to the Christmas tree and picked up the top present.

'Liberty Lovell,' he read out and he looked a bit surprised.

'Go on,' whispered Chris, and Liberty got up in his cowboy hat and walked to Father Christmas; his sisters went with him.

'Liberty Lovell, are you a good boy?' Father Christmas said, but Liberty said nothing. 'Ah well . . . nice to have you with us,' Father Christmas said, and patted the top of Liberty's hat. Then he gave presents to each of the little girls.

'Fancy them getting presents; they only come to school two days,' said Mary.

'Not fair,' said Tom, as the Lovells came back to their places.

'Linda Jones,' said Father Christmas. 'Ho, ho, are you a good girl, Linda Jones?'

'Don't open your presents now, please children,' Miss Lee said, but the Lovells were already tearing at their red

paper. Liberty looked at his pens and grinned. After that everybody opened their presents as fast as they got them. There was red paper everywhere, and Father Christmas left out the bit about being a good boy or girl and just called the names and gave out the presents as fast as he could. Then the boys started sliding up and down in the red paper like they did with autumn leaves.

'Stop that,' Father Christmas said quite sharply.

'Tea-time,' said Miss Lee, and everybody dived for the tables. Dusty and June and Chris bagged one end and they got Liberty and his sisters round it.

'They got our mum's jellies,' shouted Tom, grabbing one in each hand. 'Our mum didn't make jellies for Gypsies.'

'There's plenty of jellies your end,' shouted Chris, and Father Christmas said, 'We won't have any fighting at the Christmas party.'

'They got our mum's cake,' whispered Mary.

'We don't want it,' June said. 'Your mum makes rotten old cakes anyway.'

'Ooh, I'm telling,' whispered Mary furiously, and then somebody threw a mince-pie. Father Christmas took off his beard and there was Mr Page. 'We don't want any hooligans here,' Mr Page said sternly, and Dickie and two other Infants burst into tears.

After that everybody got on with their tea. Chris had five sardine sandwiches and every time he took one he passed one to Liberty, but Liberty's plate was always empty because he was putting sandwiches in his coat pocket. Bella put her sandwiches down the front of her jersey.

'Nice mess there's going to be in musical bumps,' whispered Dusty.

'Got your pens, have you?' Chris said, and Liberty grinned and wrote 'Liberty Lovell' on the table-cloth in blue, and then he wrote it in red.

'That's very good,' said June.

'More orange drink?' Miss Lee said. 'I don't think you should write on the table-cloth, Liberty.'

'Only paper,' Dusty said.

'How's yer chilblains, miss?' said Liberty squinting under the brim of his hat.

After tea they had games, musical bumps and grandmother's foot-steps, but the Lovells didn't play. The little girls sat under the Christmas tree and pulled the tinsel off the lower branches and wound it round themselves. Liberty wandered out to the passage and wrote his name in red on the wall, and then in blue.

'Take your balloons and go home now,' said Mrs Field. The party was over. Julie was going to phone about the Council meeting as soon as she could, Mr Beach said, and he went upstairs to wait.

'I'll get Liberty,' said Chris. Most of the children were going towards the door with their balloons, a few were picking up red paper and June and Mary were putting all the left-over cakes on to one plate. Pattella was putting left-over cakes in the front pocket of her nurse's apron, and the little girls were still playing with the tinsel under the Christmas tree.

'Where's Liberty?' said Chris.

'I don't know,' said June. Children and balloons were streaming across the playground as Chris went out to the passage. 'Liberty Lovell' was written in red on the cream wall and further down it was written in blue, and then again in red. Chris followed the trail of Liberty Lovell into the Infants class. It was dark and there was a faint click from the window. Liberty stood on the window-sill, outlined against the street lamp.

'What on earth are you doing?' said Chris.

'Just looking,' said Liberty, and he jumped down.

'Come on,' said Chris. 'Julie's going to phone about the airfield. Get your sisters up to the staffroom. I'll get the others.'

Chris and June and Dusty and Ron came pelting up the stairs just as the phone rang. Mr Beach lifted the phone and his face went pink, and Chris knew it was good news even before Mr Beach said, 'That's smashing. Congratulations. See you later, Julie.'

Mr Beach put the phone down. 'The Council are going to make the old airfield into a proper site for the Gypsies and the Gypsies can stay meanwhile.'

'Hurray,' Chris shouted.

'Where's Liberty?' said June.

They ran downstairs to the hall, but Liberty wasn't there and the little girls had gone from under the Christmas tree.

'Have you seen the Gypsy children?' Chris said.

'They just went,' Mary said. 'Liberty called them and they went.'

Chris and June and Dusty ran down the passage. The back door into the playground was open. It was dark outside and there was a track of footsteps in the frost. Chris pulled himself on to the playground wall. There was a fire on the dump and the green lorry and the blue wagon stood there in the mud. Ma and Pa Lovell crouched black against the orange flames. Liberty and his sisters were running towards them, the little girls still wrapped in silvery tinsel. Their feet clicked on the scattered tins as they ran.

The Gypsies had come back to the dump.

15 Back on the dump

'What they want to come back here for?' said June.

'Nobody's told them they're allowed to stop on the airfield,' said Chris.

'Let's go and tell them then,' said Dusty, but nobody moved. In the day the dump was just a bit of old garden with mud and trees, the children's place. But now in the darkness with the fire crackling and the strange peppery smell of cooking, it was the Gypsies' place.

'One thing, I'll be able to get the blanket all sewed together,' June said.

In the school hall several teachers and half-a-dozen children were still tidying up from the party. Mary and Linda were scraping bits of cake from the floor and Tom was sweeping up the sea of red paper with the caretaker's broom.

Chris grabbed the broom. 'You'd better get on home, hadn't you?' he said. There was a chance nobody'd notice the Gypsies as long as they kept quiet.

'What's up with you,' said Tom.

'Don't want your mum coming round, do we?' said Dusty.

'You shut up,' said Tom.

'What shall I do with this paper?' said Chris. There was a great mound of red crepe paper under the Christmas tree.

Mr Davis, the caretaker, shuffled across with two sacks. 'Put it round the dustbin.'

'I'll help you with the sacks, shall I?' said Tom.

'You ought to get home,' said Chris quickly; he didn't want Tom out in the playground. 'Isn't that right, Miss Lee? Tom and Mary ought to get on home?'

'Oh goodness, yes,' said Miss Lee. 'Your mother worries, doesn't she? Off you go and a Merry Christmas.'

Tom scowled, and Chris grinned cheerfully and carried the sacks round to the dustbins. Thames'd freeze this rate, Chris thought. The playground was slippery with frost and the wall was cold as iron under his hands. On the dump it was quiet except for the crackling of the fire. The Gypsies had gone inside the caravan. There was a faint sound close to the wall as something moved.

'Liberty, is that you?' Chris whispered, but nobody answered.

Miss Lee went for her coat and the last of the children straggled across the playground. Julie's car was parked outside.

'Merry Christmas, everybody,' Miss Lee called. 'And thank you for your help. Goodnight, Mr Davis. See you tomorrow.' It was nonsense, she thought, pulling on her gloves, but really her chilblains did seem a little less painful.

'Goodnight,' said Mr Beach. 'Goodbye.'

'Shan't see you again, shall we?' said Miss Lee shaking hands. 'The very best of luck.'

'Merry Christmas, Mr Davis,' June shouted. She and Chris and Dusty were the last up from the cloakroom. The school door clanged behind them and the bolts rattled, and one by one the lights went out.

'Quick,' said Chris. Mr Beach was already in the car. 'We got to tell them.'

'Isn't it smashing?' Julie was saying. 'Just shows what a bit of publicity does, eh? Pictures were good?'

'Fantastic,' said Mr Beach. Chris tapped on the glass, and he opened the back door. 'Hop in kids, great to see you. Drive 'em home shall we, Julie?'

'It's the Gypsies . . .' Chris began, but Julie's voice was bubbling with excitement.

'. . . this great idea. I got twelve copies of the *Mercury* and circled all the pictures with red felt pen, and pushed one through the letter-box of each person on the Housing Committee, didn't I?' Julie pursed her lips like the Chairman of the Council. '"I think we are agreed, Gentlemen, that the old airfield offers some kind of solution to the Gypsy problem?" Honestly I could have kissed the old darling, gold medal and all.' Julie turned round in her seat. 'Why don't we go out to the airfield and tell them?'

'They're back on the dump,' said Chris.

'What!' said Julie. There was a pause, and then Julie pressed the starter and backed on to the pavement and swung the car round, almost scraping the fence on the other side.

'Phew,' said Mr Beach.

Liberty crouched under the wall with the yellow bucket and stared at the stars and waited; he was used to waiting. His belly was packed tight and round as a football against his knees and that was something he wasn't used to. Beyond the wall the school door clanged shut and Gaujé voices talked in the playground and faded down the street, and Liberty waited. The squares of light in the school went out like eyes shut tight.

Liberty waited for the shuffle of the caretaker's feet and turned the little bit of yellow chalk in his pocket . . . Uncle Reuben was coming and it was Liberty should put the mark of welcome, yellow as a primrose, so he knew where to find them. They'd be gone, like the swallows, in the morning. The Gaujé had gone home just leaving the Christmas tree. Pretty glass balls, all red and green and shining bright and going to waste. A wicked shame. Fetch a lovely price in the market, Liberty thought, along with the silver tinsel.

The pale moon was a little less than round, and Liberty listened as the caretaker's feet shuffled across the playground and a door closed. There was a silence, and Liberty cupped his hands to his mouth. An owl hooted on the dump where no owl had been for thirty years.

The Lovells came over the wall quick and quiet as shadows. Only Ma took longer, gasping with the big basket and the torch in her hand. Liberty crossed the dark-striped playground. The school windows were high.

'Give us a push then,' Liberty whispered, and Pattella and Britty pushed him up the wall till he got his foot on the window-sill. He slid his knife under the metal rim of the window. A moment later he stood in the dark pit of the Infants' classroom. He sniffed the Gaujé smell of soap and cake. He was a fox, wasn't he, and this was the hen-house? Liberty unbolted the back door.

The moon shone down through the glass dome of the hall and the tinsel gleamed, and Ma's quick fingers gathered glass balls into the basket like fruit. 'Nice bit of stuff 'ere,' she said.

'Tree's ever so pretty with the lights. Tree's like a Gypsy princess,' said Britty.

'Let's see 'er then?' said Ma.

'Naw,' said Liberty. 'Leave 'er. Gaujé'll see 'er lights. Mad as magpies, you lot.'

But Pattella slipped under the tree quick as a cat and her fingers flicked the switch. The lights flashed red and blue and gold all over the tree and died like a thousand flowers.

'Us oughta brought Hopsy,' whispered Ma, and the tinsel sparkled silver in her twisting fingers. Liberty got a chair and reached up in the dark needles of the tree.

Wood was piled up high on the fire. Almost as high as the wall, Chris thought. Mrs White'd be round on her broomstick next thing; she'd only to look out the back bedroom window.

'Just asking for trouble,' said Mr Beach.

'They'll get turned off again,' said Dusty, blinking behind his spectacles.

'They don't care,' said Chris admiringly. Liberty didn't care for anybody in his cowboy hat, not teachers, or police or anybody. Gypsies were like that.

Pa Lovell was silhouetted black against the glow and Minta and Bella swung Hopsy between them, and jumped up and down with the excitement of the big fire, and Uncle Reuben coming and all the others. When Gypsies met together it was a party with singing and dancing and never mind the cold dark and the gavvers. Then Minta and Bella saw the Gaujé and they stood quite still. Julie shouted above the crackling fire. 'Mr Lovell, you got the airfield. Council's making a proper winter site of the airfield.'

Pa Lovell swung round, and his eyes were red with smoke. 'Gaujé talk is 'er?' he scowled.

'No, honestly,' said Mr Beach, pushing back his marigold hair. 'The Council has promised the old airfield. You can stop there as long as you want.'

Pa Lovell spat vigorously into the fire. 'Us stoppin' 'ere.'

'Oh, but you mustn't,' said Julie urgently.

'You'll upset everything,' said Mr Beach.

'Your fire makes black specks on Mrs Jones's washing,' said Chris. 'And they'll tow you off.'

'Who says?' Pa Lovell smiled shrewdly. A Gypsy had to

know the law and eviction orders took time. 'Us only just come.'

Behind him the little ones watched the Gaujé with dark suspicious eyes. Chris looked round for Liberty; Liberty must *make* his Pa go back. There was a circle drawn on the side of the wagon in yellow chalk. It was a circle with a dot in the middle, and there was another one on the boarded-up shops outside.

'Where's Liberty?' Chris said, and the Gypsy children stared at the fire. June bent down to the baby, Hopsy. 'Where's Liberty?' she said. The little boy's eyes slid towards the school.

'Gone to get water, has he?' whispered June, and Chris saw the quick flash of coloured lights on the Christmas tree, and remembered then, Liberty, spreadeagled at the Infants' classroom window, and the click of the latch.

'Come on,' said Chris.

The back door of the school was open, Liberty knew, and feet came running, and only Gaujé feet were loud in the dark-time. Suddenly the lights in the hall went on. The Lovells blinked, and the little girls darted under the tree, and Ma Lovell put her shawl over her basket. The bottom half of the Christmas tree was stripped of glass balls.

'What's going on?' said Mr Beach.

Liberty scowled and swung the yellow bucket. 'Come to get water, didn't us?'

'You don't come inside the school for water.'

'Just having a quick look, Guvnor,' said Ma Lovell, in a wheedling tone. 'Us'll be off now.' She jerked the basket, and the little girls scampered away like mice.

'Now look here . . .' said Mr Beach.

'What've you got in that basket?' said Julie, and Ma Lovell pulled back the shawl.

'Christmas balls. Ever so pretty,' Ma Lovell said in her sing-song voice. 'Two pence each to you, lady. Cost you five pence down the market.'

'But . . . you just took them off the tree.'

'Calling me a thief, are you?' wailed Ma Lovell, and Liberty grinned inside himself. She was a vixen was Ma, and the Gaujé were silly as hens. 'Where us get 'em, Liberty?'

'Woolworths,' said Liberty bristling.

'Woolworths, ain't 'er,' wailed Ma, and just for a moment Chris wondered whether she could be telling the truth.

'You want to watch your tongue, Gaujo. 'Er down Woolworths, 'er'll remember us.'

'Right is right and you know as well as I do . . .' Mr Beach began, but Ma Lovell was already halfway to the door. She leaned heavily on Liberty's shoulder.

'Oh, leave it,' whispered Julie. 'What do a few glass balls matter?'

'We've got to get them off the dump,' whispered Chris.

The fire was higher than ever and very hot. The Lovell children ran backwards and forwards with wood. The pile the boys had fetched with Dusty's barrow was almost finished. They'd burn the den next thing, Chris thought. There was a big black cooking pot on the fire. Liberty disappeared into the wagon.

'Awful lies she was telling,' June whispered.

'Whoppers,' said Dusty. 'Every time she opened her mouth.'

'I don't care,' said Chris. 'There's worse things than telling lies, isn't there?'

'Stealing? That's worse,' said Dusty, and Chris frowned because the Gypsies stole things too, and they were his friends, Liberty and Pattella.

Mr Beach and Julie were talking to Pa. The airfield was a great victory for the Gypsies. Now they had a place to stop, didn't they?

' 'Er's a great victory,' Pa Lovell shouted, swaying in the hot fire-light. He'd had a drink or two to keep out the cold and bring him good luck . . . And there was brother Reuben coming soon and the two cars broke and sold. 'Us wonderful grateful. Hurry up with the tea, then.'

Liberty brought the great kettle, and dark brown tea gushed into the best red and gold cups. Chris sipped, the tea was very strong and sweet and tasted of smoke. Pattella came round with a tin lid piled high with biscuits and sandwiches.

'Here, I got a bit of my mum's sponge,' Dusty whispered. 'And a lot of fluff.'

'Us wonderful grateful,' said Pa Lovell.

'But you can't stop here, Mr Lovell,' said Mr Beach urgently. 'You must go back right away.'

'Bring the gentleman something to eat, Pattella,' Pa Lovell shouted, waving his tea-cup in the air. ' 'Er's a great victory.'

Chris leant his back against the lorry wheel and stared at the fire; the others had gone. Round him the little girls found their tins and beat a rhythm with their knuckles in the darkness. First Liberty sang and then Pattella danced, whirling like a spark. She dropped down close to Chris, smelling of smoke. 'Pa's going to sing,' she said with her toothless grin. 'Pa's made a new song.'

Pa Lovell stood up and shouted into the darkness.

The Gaujé talked and talked all day,
And this is what the Gaujé say,
The whole world here belongs to us
And hell is the place for a Gypsy cuss

But us ain't going there.
But us ain't going there.

The Gaujé talked and talked all day
And this is what the Gaujé say
There's a bad luck place that us don't like
Give 'un to the Gypsies for a winter site.
But us ain't going there.
But us ain't going there.

Pa Lovell sat down, and there was silence except for the crackling of the fire. Black eyes watched the Gaujo boy. What was he going to do? Chris got slowly to his feet. He walked towards the fire and stood where Pa Lovell had stood. The Gypsies watched him. Chris didn't know what he was going to say, but suddenly he was shouting loud as Pa Lovell's song.

'We got the airfield for you, didn't we? We did everything with the Christmas play and the pictures in the paper and you ought to be pleased. We got the airfield, didn't we? Why aren't you going there?'

For a moment the Lovells stared at Chris in silence, and then Pa said, 'Can't sell us Christmas flowers out there.'

' 'Er's a bad luck place,' said Ma Lovell. 'Wind like the devil's breath.'

' 'Er's weasels,' said Liberty.

'Us ain't going there,' said Ma.

' "Hairs growin' on a diamond first",' said Liberty.

'But you can't stay here. You'll get turned off again,' Chris shouted. His eyes pricked with anger and hurt, and suddenly there was a rumbling noise from the street. A dark red lorry was coming across the pavement on to the dump and there was a wagon behind it. Uncle Reuben had seen the yellow sign of welcome on the boarded-up shops outside. A great cheer went up from the Lovells, 'Uncle Reuben, Uncle Reuben.'

Liberty ran across, and the lorry doors were flung open and dogs barked and lots more children jumped out – Lovells all of them, Uncle Reuben's children.

There was a lot of shrieking and shouting, and then Uncle Reuben's family came round the fire and there was tea, and Ma Lovell stirred the great black stew-pot and Pattella danced and Liberty sang a song.

Chris sat with his back to the lorry wheel but the Lovells had forgotten him. They had forgotten their troubles too, the police and being towed off and the cold and nowhere to stop and the Gaujé.

Bit of good luck and life was a party.

16 A place to stop

It was time to go. Already the first traffic was purring in the dark-time beyond the dump. Liberty flicked the red curtain. There was a rim of snow at the wagon window, and snow-flakes floating down like white feathers.

Liberty put on his hat and fumbled with the Queenie stove. It was cold in the wagon under the thick blanket of snow but there was glowing red in the stove's heart still. Pa and Ma awoke in the big bed and in the darkness underneath the little girls stirred and whimpered like a nest of kittens. Liberty lit the lamp, the light caught the tinsel and the crystal door knob and the flash-bulbs, silver blue; prettier things than any Gaujo had in his grey house, Liberty thought. Lamp-light gleamed on the snow from Uncle Reuben's wagon. All the Lovells were going, it was time to go.

'See us out,' Pa said, coughing white in the dark air. He got into the lorry cabin and Ma and Hopsy and the little girls scrambled after him, huddling close together and shivering. Across the dump Uncle Reuben and Aunt Bella and their children jumped down from their wagon and ran across the snow to the lorry. The lorry engines coughed and revved.

Liberty walked across the dump. The snow muffled his feet and flew icy in his face. There was a thin layer on the grey pavement and a car slid by, white and quiet as a ghost. The traffic lights winked red and green in the dark.

' 'Er's all right,' Liberty shouted and waved his arms, and the lorries revved and rumbled slowly forward with their wagons. The yellow chalk circle on the boarded-up shops caught Liberty's eye; 'Gypsies are welcome here' the sign said, the welcome sign for Uncle Reuben. Liberty frowned and took the chalk from his pocket and put two lines underneath. 'Gypsies are not welcome here' the sign said now, like the cold eyes of the Gaujé.

The lorries came towards him. Pa's lorry bounced across the pavement first and on to the road, and Uncle Reuben's followed and Liberty shouted, 'Right and right again.' He looked back at the dump and the black tracks in the white snow and the dark of the Gaujé houses round. It was the Gaujo boy, Chris, taught him to write his name and waved that first morning, and now they were going. Liberty raised his arm and waved, but there was nobody to see.

Pa waited by the lights, and Liberty ran down the road through the falling snow and scrambled up.

It was snowing and still dark, but the caravans had gone. Chris stared miserably out of the bedroom window. The fire patch made a black smudge under the snow and the tracks of the wheels were veiled over. All that, and then they didn't even want the airfield, Chris thought sadly. The Gypsies had nowhere to go and he had written his letter and Julie had taken her pictures and they'd got the airfield and then the Gypsies didn't even want it. It was all wasted . . .

'You getting up or aren't you?' Mum called up the stairs. June had gone down already. Chris sighed and pulled on his jeans.

'Holds me up, this late breakfast,' Mum said, with bacon

and tomatoes sizzling in the pan. 'You get up the proper time, my lad.'

'Holidays, isn't it?' Chris said sulkily.

'It's snowing,' said June.

'Poor old dog doesn't like the snow, does he?' Dad said, and Rags thumped his tail.

'All you care about, that old dog,' said Chris angrily. 'People are more important than dogs, aren't they?'

'What's wrong with that?' Dad said. 'He's a good old dog, isn't he?'

'Gypsies have gone any road,' Mum said.

'All that din last night, singing and shouting.'

'Didn't like the airfield, did they?' June said.

'It was a bad luck place,' said Chris. Liberty didn't mind anything except bad luck.

'Lucky to get any place,' said Mum.

Dad went to work and Mum washed up the breakfast things and Chris just sat by the fire. He had nothing to do, nothing he wanted to do.

June had something to do. She sat at the kitchen table making Christmas cards, sticking silver stars on pieces of paper. June was like that. 'Don't call these Christmas cards do you?' said Chris scornfully.

'Leave her,' said Mum. She looked at Chris, 'Take the old dog out, why don't you?'

It was grey outside and fat white snowflakes floated past the kitchen window. 'Too blinkin' cold,' said Chris.

'Where's Dusty got to then?' Mum said. 'Go and find Dusty.'

'Goes down the market Saturdays,' said Chris. 'Helps his auntie down the market.'

'Cheer up, it's Christmas time,' said Mum.

Chris put on his coat and went out in the softly falling

snow. He wandered along the pavement. The curtain twitched at number twenty-five; it was Tom. Been friends since the Infants, hadn't they, but Chris didn't want Tom, not now.

The snow was thick on the dump, and Chris blinked at the clean whiteness. The den was covered over like an igloo. There was the yellow chalk circle on the boarded-up shops and two lines underneath. Chris rubbed it to a round smudge with his sleeve. The Gypsies had gone and everything had been wasted.

In Wood Lane Primary School the light was on in Class Six.

'Hallo, Chris,' said Miss Lee. She was taking pictures off the classroom walls, prising out the drawing pins carefully. Miss Lee liked to make a fresh start each term. 'Come to help me, have you?'

'All right,' said Chris, and he ripped the Gypsy pictures off the wall, tearing the corners.

'I was going to leave those,' Miss Lee said. She blinked at Chris. 'Those are new. Is something the matter?' Chris swallowed, and suddenly the words came tumbling out.

'Why didn't they go there, miss? Sorry for them, weren't we, because they had nowhere to stop, and we did everything and the Christmas play and I wrote this letter with all the names, only nobody signed it really, only me, and we got the airfield for them, didn't we, so why didn't they go there?' He broke off with a strangled sob. 'I'll give 'em weasels.'

'People don't always like being helped,' said Miss Lee slowly. 'Sometimes it hurts their pride.' Chris sniffed. What had the Gypsies got to be proud of, he wondered.

'The airfield won't be wasted,' said Miss Lee. 'The Council's going to make a proper winter site for twelve caravans. That's twelve Gypsy families have got somewhere to stop.'

'Who cares about twelve families?' said Chris blowing his nose. 'Liberty and Pattella we did it for.'

The snow came softly down all day; it lay thick and white on the grey roofs and the tops of walls. In the afternoon the snow stopped and the street lamps clicked on, turning the sky mauve. Chris went out again. On the dump nobody had walked yet, and he sunk his foot in the clean snow whiteness; it came to the top of his shoe. It was two inches thick at least.

He walked across to the old apple tree. Snow lay like a white blanket over the den. Chris stepped on to the bare earth inside.

'We were going to live here summertime,' he muttered,

and suddenly a fierce anger boiled inside him and he kicked at the wall of boxes with all his might. The wall collapsed; battered boxes lay in the snow.

Chris ran down Kings' Street and into the High Street. He ran on and on . . . past the Co-op and the terrace and The Bull . . .

'Hey . . . Chris.' Chris stopped running. Julie's small car slid into the kerb. Mr Beach sat beside Julie. He had a coat with thick fur down the front and a lot of red and black embroidery.

'Where you off to then?' said Julie, and Chris gulped for breath and couldn't speak.

'Looks like a boiled lobster, doesn't he?' said Mr Beach. 'Hop in.'

'What for?' said Chris, but he got in the back. 'You don't care, do you?'

'Care about what?' said Julie, and she turned to look at him, and her blue eyes were very clear with dark rings round the blue.

'Just so long as you got a good story,' said Chris.

'That's not fair,' said Mr Beach.

'It's fair enough,' said Julie. 'I wanted a story but I wanted to help too. What did you want, Chris?'

'Me?'

'Didn't you want to make up for that window?' Julie said softly, and Chris looked away. 'Where we going then?'

'Down the High Street and then left and left and then right,' said Mr Beach.

'What's the good of that?' said Chris. 'Didn't like the old airfield, did they? All weasels and devil's breath, isn't it?'

'Hush,' said Julie. 'Hush.'

The sky was dark violet as they left the High Street. Snow lay in the front gardens and outside the town even the road was white. They turned into the narrow lane that led to the airfield. Julie switched off the lights and the car went slowly down the lane.

'Come on,' said Julie. She parked the car.

'Quiet,' whispered Mr Beach. Snow muffled their footsteps as they trudged down the lane. It was quite dark now. A dog barked and somebody shouted, and then Chris heard the harsh cackle of Ma Lovell's laugh, and through the hedge he saw them, the caravans and lorries and a fire and sparks going up in the darkness and the Gypsies crouched close like black crows. Somebody was singing.

Chris scrambled up the bank. 'It's them, the whole lot of them, it's Liberty,' he whispered.

'Look out,' whispered Mr Beach. 'Don't let them see you.'

'But they said . . .'

'A Gypsy doesn't want to be grateful to a Gaujo,' whispered Mr Beach.

'They like their secrets,' Julie whispered. 'They don't like any Gaujo knowing where they are.'

'It's like birds,' said Chris wonderingly. 'Birds leave their nests if you look at the eggs.'

'Yes,' said Julie.

'And they really like the airfield?' said Chris.

'It's somewhere to stop, isn't it?' said Mr Beach. 'They'll stop here till the picking starts.'

It was Julie flung the first snowball and it hit Chris smack in the chest, and then they were all running up the road, feet thudding and snowballs flying in the dark air.

Julie turned the car. It was getting colder and the snow crunched crisply. Chris wound down his window an inch and the air blew cold on his hot face. There was baked beans for tea and old June doing her Christmas cards and the den was still there, at least it would be when he got Tom and

Dusty round the dump. Tomorrow was Sunday and there was never anything to do on a Sunday afternoon. They'd make a real good den. Might even sleep there summertime, only Tom's mum'd never let him. 'Hair growin' on a diamond first', Chris thought, and he smiled. Nothing was wasted.

' 'Er's a car in the lane,' Liberty said, and the singing stopped. The Gypsies listened to the sounds of the night, and the fire crackled and away in the woods an owl hooted.

'Ain't nothing,' said Ma Lovell, pulling her shawl round Hopsy, asleep in her lap. Her voice was softer now they had somewhere to stop.

Liberty stood up to sing, shouting loud as he could into the darkness. Good luck was come with a place to stop all wintertime, and never mind the weasel whickered. Aunt Bella was come for the baby's birth and that was good luck, and the two cars broke and the scrap sold and that was good luck, and one more to fetch and break and that was good luck. It was Christmas too and the Gaujé didn't know where they were and that was best luck of all, and in the spring they'd move on because a Gypsy had to follow the sun round and round the earth.